LEARNING TURKISH
IN 10 EASY STEPS

Henri Adato

Learning Turkish in 10 Easy Steps

Onex
Weston, Connecticut

© 2009 Henri Adato. All rights reserved. No part of this book may be reproduced or transmitted in any form or by any means, electronic or mechanical, including photocopying, recording or by any information storage and retrieval system, without the written permission of the publisher.

ISBN-13: 978-0615675381
ISBN-10: 0615675387

CONTENTS

INTRODUCTION..1

1 SOME PRINCIPLES OF THE TURKISH LANGUAGE..............1
    A FEW GENERAL PRINCIPLES..1
    THE ALPHABET AND SOUND OF THE LETTERS...................1
    VOWELS...2
    PRINCIPLES ABOUT VERBS..2
    WHAT'S AHEAD..3

2 VERBS..5
    THE FUNDAMENTAL FORMS (TENSES)................................5
        THE INFINITIVE..5
        THE (SIMPLE) PRESENT TENSE.....................................6
            The form..6
            The negative..6
            ...and the Person...6
        THE (SIMPLE) PAST TENSE..7
            The form..7
            The negative..7
            ...and the Person...8
        THE PRESENT PERFECT AND PAST PERFECT TENSE...........8
            The form..8
            PRESENT PERFECT FORM...9
            PAST PERFECT FORM..9
            The negative..9
            ...and the Person...9
        THE FUTURE TENSE...10
            The form..10
            The negative..10
            ...and the Person...10
        THE PAST PROGRESSIVE (FUTURE CONDITIONAL)..........11
            The form..11
            The negative..11
            ...and the Person...11
        THE ONCE-UPON-A-TIME FORM.......................................12
            The form..12
            The negative..12

...and the Person...12
A QUICK RETURN TO THE SIMPLE PRESENT FORM...........**13**
   The negative..13
THE PRESENT CONTINUOUS FORM..................................**14**
   The form..14
   The negative..14
   ...and the Person...14
THE PAST CONTINUOUS TENSE...**15**
   The form..15
   The negative..15
   ...and the Person...15
WE TAKE A BREAK TO LOOK AT WHAT'S NEXT.............**15**

3 A REVIEW OF WHAT WE LEARNED SO FAR.............17

4 REFINING AND BUILDING ON WHAT WE LEARNED..........19

FIRST LET'S REVIEW AND ADD SOME BACKGROUND KNOWLEDGE...**19**
MAKING ADJUSTMENTS TO WHAT WE LEARNED..............**20**
  APPLYING TONE COORDINATION TO SUFFIXES..................**20**:
    TONE COORDINATION: THE NEGATION SUFFIX......................20
    TONE COORDINATION: THE VERB FORMS AND TENSES........20
    The Infinitive...20
    The Simple Present...20
    The Simple Past..21
    The Present Perfect Form..22
    The Past Perfect Form..23
    The Future Tense..23
    The Past Progressive (Future Conditional).......................23
    The Once-Upon-a-Time Form..24
    SUMMARIZING WHAT YOU KNOW SO FAR............................24
    TONE COORDINATION: THE PERSON....................................24
  COMBINING SUFFIXES SMOOTHLY.......................................**25**
NOT ONLY "FIRST PERSON" : LEARNING THE ADVERBS........**26**
A QUICK LOOK AT TURKISH LETTERS................................**28**

5 TWO NEW FORMS: THE INTERROGATIVE AND THE CONDITIONAL...29

THE INTERROGATIVE FORM...**29**
   Tone Coordination..29
   Applying to All Tenses...30
THE CONDITIONAL (IF) FORM..**31**

	ONCE AGAIN, WHAT'S NEXT?..34

6 PERSONS..35

THE PERSON..35
WHERE DO WE USE THE PERSON..35

7 THE VERB "TO BE"..37

"TO BE" IN TURKISH..37
VERB FORMS (TENSES)..37
    The infinitive..37
    ...And other tenses..37
    The (simple) present tense..38
    The (simple) past tense..38
    The perfect..38
    The future tense..38
    The past progressive (future conditional)..38
    The once-upon-a-time form..38
    The present continuous..38
    The past continuous...39
    Correct placement of the "to be" suffix..39
THE REFLECTIVE FORM..40
" HAVE" and "NOT HAVE"..40

8 USING ARTICLES "at" "to" "into" "from" "of" "with", THE WORDS "This", "That" AND THE POSSESSIVE.....41

USING AN ARTICLE..41
    ADDING WORDS TO OUR - SO FAR - LIMITED VOCABULARY............41
    THE ARTICLE "A"..41
    THE ARTICLE "THE"..42
THE WORDS "this", "that"..43
THE "to", "at", "into", "in" AND "from", "of", "with" WORDS...43
    "to" ,"at", "into" and "in" : using "to"..43
    "to", "at", "into" and "in" : using "at"..44
    "to" ,"at", "in" and "into" : using "in"..45
    "to" ,"at", "in" and "into" : using "into"..45
    And now "from"..46
    With..47
THE POSSESSIVE..48
THE PREPOSITION "OF"..49
HAVE and NOT HAVE..50

9 THE PLURAL 51

10 WHO, WHERE, AND WHAT/WHICH/WHEN/HOW 52

WHO 52
WHERE 52
    Where (with the verb "be") 53
    Where (to) 53
    Where (from) 53
WHAT, WHICH, WHEN, HOW 53
WHEN 54
HOW 54

11 USING YOUR NEW LANGUAGE 55

SEQUENCING 55
VOCABULARY 55
MAKING PHRASES 59

INTRODUCTION

THE WAY THIS TEXT TEACHES

This text teaches Turkish by initially outlining the architecture and basic principles of the Turkish language. While doing so we will make some simplifications which will allow us to focus on easily learning these basic principles.

Once the basic principles have been made clear, we will then generalize those principles showing the variations as they may apply to different cases. Although without these additions to the basic principles the language would be imperfect if not flawed, this gradual approach to correctness allows the reader to easily focus on and thus quickly learn the fundamental principles.

For example the past tense suffix is often *di* but also *ti* in certain cases. We will initially use *di* universally, eventually showing where the suffix has a slightly different form such as *ti* , *du* and some other forms.

HOW TO USE THIS TEXT

This text is accompanied by an exercise and answer book. The exercise book adds to the knowledge of this text and therefore not only helps you review and remember what is learned here but also complements the learning provided in this text. You are therefore encouraged to use the exercise book together with the text.

This text is rather complete and except for the vocabulary and certain special forms and expressions covers the whole of the Turkish language. You can therefore use the text to learn in stages:

      If you want to, in the shortest period of time, manage to simply express yourself you can, at first, just go through the sections indexed in black. You can later complete your learning with the indexed sections shown in grey.

The text is organized in ten learning steps and eleven sections (section 3 is essentially a table summarizing what is learned in steps 1 and 2).

1 SOME PRINCIPLES OF THE TURKISH LANGUAGE

A FEW GENERAL PRINCIPLES

In Turkish the root words are mostly monosyllabic.
Conjugation is done using suffixes rather than with separate words.
The suffixes have a basic form, but in order to make the pronunciations smoother the suffixes take on slight variations depending on the intonation of the word they tag onto.

THE ALPHABET AND SOUND OF THE LETTERS

We will only look at the letters used in the examples in the next sections. The complete alphabet will be explained further down.

Turkish letter	Corresponding English letter(s)	sounds as in English word:
a	a	art
e	e	hey (hay) or less
g	g	glad
ğ	w	prolongs the preceding vowel as in slowly
ı	i	the (as in "the book")
i	i	visit (but may be closer to he)
o	o	or
ö	ea	learn , sir
ş	sh	shame
u	oo	foot , who
ü	(u)	Ursula

TABLE 1.1
Partial set of letter phonetics

VOWELS

Vowels are broken down into two groups:
- the **thin vowels**
- the **thick** (deep sounding) **vowels**

The **thin vowels** are: e i ö ü

The **thick vowels** are: a ı o u

Normally, a Turkish word contains either only thin or only deep vowels but not a mix of both.

PRINCIPLES ABOUT VERBS

In Turkish most words, and therefore verbs, are, in their root form, monosyllabic.
For example:

sev	=	like (love)
dön	=	turn (return)
gel	=	come

The tense, the person, and negation if any, are molded into the verb with suffixes.
Suffixes are added to verbs in a preset order.

The first suffix placed is that (if it is the case) of negation.
The negation suffix is *me*.

Example:

sev	=	like
sev*me*	=	...not like (don't like)
gel	=	come
gel*me*	=	...not come (don't come)
dön	=	return
dön*me*	=	...not return

The second suffix is the tense.
Let's take the case of the simple past tense. The suffix for the simple past tense is *di*.

Example:

sev	=	like
sev*di*	=	liked
gel	=	come
gel*di*	=	came

The third suffix is the person. Let's take "I" as the person. The suffix for I is ***im***.

Example:

sev*di*	=	liked
sev*diim*	=	I liked
gel*di*	=	came
gel*diim*	=	I came

VERB	negate	tense	person	
sev		di	im	I liked
sev	me	di	im	I did not like
gel		di	im	I came
gel	me	di	im	I did not come

TABLE 1.2
Verbs With Negation, Tense and Person Suffixes

WHAT'S AHEAD

Now that we have seen the basic principles affecting verbs (using the simple past tense as a guide) we can move on to applying that to all the forms of verbs, that is, all tenses.

Our first task will be to learn how to use Turkish verbs, to build the equivalent of small phrases.

As a phrase to aim for let us think of:

"I did not come to the village"

Let us, however, put this phrase aside for now and proceed with general principles regarding verbs.

2 VERBS

THE FUNDAMENTAL FORMS (TENSES)

In this chapter we will look at the different forms verbs take on to represent the tense.

THE INFINITIVE

The infinitive form of a verb in English leads the verb with *to*.
For example the infinitive of the verb
        like
is   to like

In Turkish we use the suffix **mek**

For example:

sev	=	like (love)
sev*mek*	=	to like (love)
gel	=	come
gel*mek*	=	to come

And, of course the negative form is very easy in Turkish because the standard negation rule applies just the same here too.
In English the negative uses *not to* instead of *to*.
For example the negative of
        to like
is   not to like

Remember, In Turkish the negative is obtained with the suffix **me**.

For example

sev	=	like
sev*me*	=	don't like

And so it is with the infinitive

sevmek	=	to like
sev*me*mek	=	not to like

You can see that the (infinitive) suffix **mek** can be added to the basic form of the verb and to the negative form of the verb.

Note that the suffix sequencing rule keeps applying:
>the **first suffix**, if used, is the **negation**
>the **second** is the **tense**.

Also note that, just as in English, **the infinitive does not use a person**. Therefore, our summary table below will not have anything in the "person" column.

VERB	negate	tense infinitive	person	
sev		mek		to like
sev	me	mek		not to like
gel		mek		to come
gel	me	mek		not to come

TABLE 2.1
The Suffix for the Infinitive

THE (SIMPLE) PRESENT TENSE

<u>The form</u>
In English the present tense of a verb has the same form as the root form of the verb. Thus when we say *I come* we are using the basic form of the verb *come* .

In Turkish the present form of the verb has a suffix. This suffix is *er* .

For example:
>sev = like (basic form of verb)
>sev*er* = like (present form, such as in "I like")

<u>The negative</u>
We shall avoid dealing with the negative form of the present tense. This is because, with the simple present tense, the suffix takes on an exceptional form and we want to avoid dealing with exceptions right now.

<u>...and the Person</u>
Remember, from Chapter 1 SOME PRINCIPLES OF THE TURKISH LANGUAGE, that the suffix for the person "I" is "im" in Turkish.

Hence:

sev	=	like (basic form of verb)
sever	=	like (present form of verb)
sever*im*	=	I like

VERB	negate	tense present	person	
sev		er	im	I like
sev	me	will be dealt with further down		
gel		er	im	I come
gel	me	will be dealt with further down		

TABLE 2.2
The Suffix for the Simple Present Tense

THE (SIMPLE) PAST TENSE

<u>The form</u>
In English the simple past tense form of regular verbs is obtained by adding *(e)d* to the end of the verb. And so the past tense form of the verb *like* is *liked*. (There are, as we know other forms of past tense such as *run ran; bring: brought...*).

In Turkish the simple past tense is obtained by adding the suffix **di**.

For example:

sev	=	like
sev*di*	=	liked

<u>The negative</u>
The negative, as usual, is obtained with the suffix **me**.

Example:

sev	=	like
sev*me*	=	don't like

and so it is with the simple past tense:

sevdi	=	liked
sev*me*di	=	didn't like

...and the Person
And again, remember from Chapter 1 that the suffix for the person "I" is "im" in Turkish.

Hence:
sev	=	like
sevdi	=	liked
sevdi*im*	=	I liked
sevmedi*im*	=	I didn't like

VERB	negate	tense	person	
sev		di	im	I liked
sev	me	di	im	I did not like
gel		di	im	I came
gel	me	di	im	I did not come

TABLE 2.3
The Suffix for the Simple Past Tense

THE PRESENT PERFECT AND PAST PERFECT TENSE

The form
This tense uses *have* (present participle) and *had* (past participle) in conjunction with the basic verb. Examples to this form are:

        I have liked
        I have come   (present perfect)

and   I had liked
        I had come   (past perfect)

PRESENT PERFECT FORM:

Turkish does not distinguish between simple past   (liked)
and present perfect   (have liked)

The Turkish equivalent for both forms uses the suffix *di*.

Hence:
	sev*di*	=	liked
and	sev*di*	=	have liked

PAST PERFECT FORM:

In Turkish the perfect is formed by adding in front of the simple past suffix *di* the suffix *miş* thus forming the combined suffix *mişdi*. In actual use, though, the suffix takes the form **mişti** (the *d* is "softened" into a *t*.)

For example:
    sev   =   like
    sev*mişti*   =   had liked

The negative
We shall now remember that the negative form of the verb is obtained with the suffix *me* as the very first addition to the basic form of the verb.

Example:
    sev   =   liked
    sev*me*   =   don't like

And so it is with the past perfect tense

    sevmişti   =   had liked
    sev*me*mişti   =   had not liked

...and the Person
And again, remember from Chapter 1 that the suffix for the person "I" is "im" in Turkish.

Hence:
    sev   =   liked
    sevmişti   =   had liked
    sevmişti*im*   =   I had liked

and, of course, you can add the person to the negative form too:

    sevmemişti   =   had not liked
    sevmemişti*im*   =   I had not liked

As always, you notice that the suffix sequence is as follows:
    first the negation (if used)
    second the tense
    third the person

VERB	negate	tense	person	
sev		mişti	im	I had liked
sev	me	mişti	im	I had not liked
gel		mişti	im	I had come
gel	me	mişti	im	I had not come

TABLE 2.4
The Suffix for the Past Perfect Tense

THE FUTURE TENSE

<u>The form</u>
Here too the tense is expressed with a suffix. The suffix for the future tense is *ecek*.

For example:
        sev   =   like
        sev*ecek*   =   will like

<u>The negative</u>
Similarly with the negative:

        sev*me*   =   not like
        sev*me*ecek   =   will not like

<u>...and the Person</u>
And we can add the first person:

        sevecek   =   will like
        sevecek*im*   =   I will like
        sevmeecek   =   will not like
        sevmeecek*im*   =   I will not like

VERB	negate	tense	person	
sev		ecek	im	I will like
sev	me	ecek	im	I will not like
gel		ecek	im	I will come
gel	me	ecek	im	I will not come

TABLE 2.5
Suffix for the Future Tense

THE PAST PROGRESSIVE (FUTURE CONDITIONAL)

The form
The future conditional, in English, takes the form *was going to* .
The Turkish form is made with the suffix *ecekdi* . To add a little precision we should say that the form is really made of the suffix *ecek* with the added word *idi* . However this form is practically never used and we'll stay with the united suffix *ecekdi* . In fact the letter t is substituted for the d for a "softer" pronunciation – ***ecekti*** .

For example:

sev	=	like
sev*ecekti*	=	was going to like

The negative
Similarly with the negative:

sevme	=	not like
sev*me*ecekti	=	was not going to like

...and the Person
And we can add the first person:

sevecekti	=	was going to like
sevecekti*im*	=	I was going to like
sevmeecekti	=	was not going to like
sevmeecekti*im*=		I was not going to like

VERB	negate	tense	person	
sev		ecekti	im	I was going to like
sev	me	ecekti	im	I was not going to like
gel		ecekti	im	I was going to come
gel	me	ecekti	im	I was not going to come

TABLE 2.6
Suffix for the Future Conditional Form

THE ONCE-UPON-A-TIME FORM

<u>The form</u>
The English form is *used to* as in *I used to like...*
The Turkish form is obtained with the suffix **erdi**.

For example:
- sev = like
- sev*erdi* = used to like

<u>The negative</u>
Similarly (?) with the negative:

- sev*me* = do not like
- sev*me*erdi (?) = used not to like (didn't use to like)

Well, not quite. We hit here upon a small exception. In the negative the suffix erdi changes form slightly, and becomes:
ezdi

So now we can come back to forming our negative:

- sev*me* = do not like
- sev*me*ezdi = used not to like (didn't use to like)

<u>...and the Person</u>
And we can add the first person:

- severdi = used to like
- severdi*im* = I used to like
- sevmeezdi = used not to like (didn't use to like)
- sevmeezdi*im* = I used not to like (I didn't use to like)

VERB	negate	tense	person	
gel		erdi	im	I used to come
gel	me	ezdi	im	I used not to come
sev		erdi	im	I used to like
sev	me	ezdi	im	I used not to like

TABLE 2.7
Suffix for the Once-Upon-a-Time Form

Note: This form is also used in Turkish when meaning "would..." as in "would run..." or "would go running...". This is further explained in the Advanced Text.

A QUICK RETURN TO THE SIMPLE PRESENT FORM:

If you briefly recap the Simple Present Form explained above you will notice that we omitted the negative because it took on an exceptional form. We shall now learn the negative form of this tense.

<u>The negative</u>
As you recap this tense you will see that the required suffix was e*r* .
For example:

   sev   = like (basic form of verb)
   sever = like (present form, such as in "I like")

The negative for the verb
   sev
is, as you know
   sev*me*
When tagged to the negative, the tense suffix is of a slightly different form, where instead of
   er
it takes the form:
   ez, (same as the once-upon-a-time form, just shown above).

Thus:
   sev   = like (basic form of verb)
   sev*er* = like (present form, such as in "I like")
   sevme*ez* = not like (such as in "she does not like...")

This form has other exceptions:
 In the case of the first person that we have always used so far, the suffix is altogether dropped.
  This is how it happens:
   sev*er*   = like (present form, such as in "I like")
   sevme*ez* = not like (such as in "she does not like...")
   sevmee*zim* (?)
 no, it really looks as follows:
   sevme_*im* = I do not like
 and since pronouncing *sevmeim* is quite cumbersome the first person takes an even bigger shortcut and drops the *i* too, to end up with the "correct" form (for the first person only) of:
   sevme*m*   = I do not like

THE PRESENT CONTINUOUS FORM

The form
The English for this tense takes the form "...*ing*" such as in "*I am coming...*"
The Turkish form is obtained with the suffix ***iyor***.

For example:

sev	=	like
sev*iyor*	=	liking (am, are)

The negative
As usual we can use the negative form:

seviyor	=	liking
sev*me*iyor	=	not liking

...and the Person
And we can add the first person:

seviyor	=	liking
seviyor*im*	=	I am liking
sevmeiyor	=	not liking
sevmeiyor*im*	=	I am not liking

VERB	negate	tense	person	
sev		iyor	im	I am liking
sev	me	iyor	im	I am not liking
gel		iyor	im	I am coming
gel	me	iyor	im	I am not coming

TABLE 2.8
Suffix for the Present Continuous Tense

THE PAST CONTINUOUS TENSE

<u>The form</u>
The English for this tense takes the form "*...ing*" such as in "*I was coming...*"
The Turkish form is obtained with the suffix *iyordi* .

For example:
        sev   =   like
        sev*iyordi*   =   liking (was, were)

<u>The negative</u>
As usual we can use the negative form:

        seviyordi   =   liking
        sev*me*iyordi =   not liking

<u>...and the Person</u>
And we can add the first person:

        seviyordi   =   liking
        seviyordi*im*   =   I was liking
        sevmeiyordi   =   not liking
        sevmeiyordi*im*=   I was not liking

VERB	negate	tense	person	
sev		iyordi	im	I was liking
sev	me	iyordi	im	I was not liking
gel		iyordi	im	I was coming
gel	me	iyordi	im	I was not coming

TABLE 2.9
Suffix for the Past Continuous Tense

WE TAKE A BREAK TO LOOK AT WHAT'S NEXT

We have almost covered every major aspect of verbs. "Almost", because **there are seven more forms** three of which we'll learn in this Basic Book (and the remaining in the Advanced Book).

In the next two chapters **we will recap** what we have learned so far, **and refine** (or even make adjustments or small corrections to) what we learned.

Then in the following chapters we will address three more forms, namely:
- The interrogative form. (As in "did you like?")
- The conditional form – "if", "had". (As in "if I liked", "had I liked")
  where Turkish differentiates the context of these forms
- The verb "to be" and its uses.

and will also learn:
- The persons (adverbs)
- Using articles "at" "to" "into" "from" "of", the words "this", "that" and the possessive
- The words "who" "where" "what" "when"

and then
- The plurals
- The sequence of words in sentences

At that point, subject to expanding your vocabulary – some of which will happen as you perform the exercises that come with this text – you will be in a position to express yourself quite well in Turkish.

There will remain some more involved forms to learn in order to perfect your Turkish but these and other topics are best left to be dealt with in the Advanced Book. Some of the forms addressed in the Advanced Book are:

- The "apparently" form. Turkish uses a simple suffix to imply "apparently" or "appears that" such as in "he apparently knew ..."
- The two reflective forms. As in "he made me like..." and "I am liked..."
- More on the once-upon-a-time form (would have...)
- The "able" form. As in I was able to like..."
- The "let us" form. As in "let's like..."

Before moving into those slightly more esoteric forms let us consolidate our work up to now. We will therefore review what we have learned, and also improve on it.

3 A REVIEW OF WHAT WE LEARNED SO FAR

We have, so far, seen:

1. how to form the tenses
2. how to form the negative
3. how to add the first person suffix

Table 3.1 below summarizes what we learned.

TENSE (FORM)	EXAMPLE IN ENGLISH WITH FIRST PERSON	TURKISH TENSE SUFFIX	EXAMPLE IN TURKISH WITH FIRST PERSON	AND WITH NEGATIVE
Infinitive	to like	mek	sevmek	sevmemek
Simple Present	I like	er	severim	sevmem (1)
Simple Past	I liked	di	sevdiim	sevmediim
Present Perfect	I have liked	indistinct from simple past		
Past Perfect	I had liked	mişti	sevmiştiim	sevmemiştiim
Future	I will like	ecek	sevecekim	sevmeecekim
Future Conditional	I was going to like	ecekti	sevecektiim	sevmeecektiim
Once-Upon-a-Time	I used to come	irdi	gelirdiim	gelmeezdiim (2)

(1) Special case: with this negative the tense suffix is dropped; the first person "im" suffix becomes only "m".
(2) Special case: in the negative the tense suffix "ir" mutates to "ez".

Table 3.1
Reviewing All Tenses.

4 REFINING AND BUILDING ON WHAT WE LEARNED

We shall now proceed with making some adjustments to what we learned so far. After doing that we will quickly learn how to use our verbs with all the persons.

FIRST LET'S REVIEW AND ADD SOME BACKGROUND KNOWLEDGE

If you remember from the first section, the Turkish vowels are broken down into two groups: the **thin vowels** and the **thick** (deep sounding) **vowels**.

The thin vowels are: e i ö ü

The thick vowels are: a ı o u

Normally, a Turkish word contains either only thin or only deep vowels but not a mix of both.
We will now apply this principle to the suffixes which we already know.

But **first let us learn a few new Turkish words:**

    We already know:
sev	=	like (love)
gel	=	come
dön	=	turn (return)

    Here are some new ones:
it	=	push
düş	=	fall

    You notice that all the words above have **thin** vowels.

    And now some more new words:
at	=	throw
kır	=	break
koş	=	run
tut	=	catch/hold

    You notice that the words in this second group have **thick** vowels

(Look up the table in Section 1 to see how to pronounce the words. In fact keep a copy of this table in sight as we move along this section in order to get the correct pronunciation.)

MAKING ADJUSTMENTS TO WHAT WE LEARNED

APPLYING TONE COORDINATION TO SUFFIXES:

TONE COORDINATION: THE NEGATION SUFFIX

We learned that the negation suffix is *me*. The truth is that the negation suffix takes the form of *me* or of *ma*.
The suffix is *me* when the vowel in the root is thin,
The suffix is *ma* when the vowel in the root is thick
Let us apply this rule to the words we now know:

sev	sevme	at	atma
it	itme	kır	kırma
dön	dönme	koş	koşma
düş	düşme	tut	tutma

TONE COORDINATION: THE VERB FORMS AND TENSES

The Infinitive:

The same rule applies. the suffix for the infinitive is not uniformly *mek*.
The suffix is *mek* when the vowel in the root is thin,
The suffix is *mak* when the vowel in the root is thick.

sev	sevmek	at	atmak
it	itmek	kır	kırmak
dön	dönmek	koş	koşmak
düş	düşmek	tut	tutmak

The Simple Present:

Here too the rule is simple and is the same as for the infinitive:
The suffix is *er* when the vowel in the root is thin,
The suffix is *ar* when the vowel in the root is thick.

This tense also has some less common forms where the thin vowel suffix takes, in some cases, the forms of ir or ür ; and the thick vowel suffix the form of ır or ur . We will, for now, leave aside these variations (but, to satisfy your curiosity know that these forms are sometimes used when the last consonant of the root word is the letter "l", "n" or "r").

sev	sever	at	atar
it	iter	kır	kırar
dön	döner	koş	koşar
düş	düşer	tut	tutar

The Simple Past:

The rule is universal but slightly complex. Let us say initially that:
The suffix is *di* or *dü* when the verb has a thin vowel –
   di when the thin vowel is **e** or **i**
   dü when the thin vowel is **ö** or **ü**
The suffix is *dı* or *du* when the verb has a thick vowel -
   dı when the thick vowel is **a** or **ı**
   du when the thick vowel is **o** or **u**

sev	sevdi	at	attı
it	itti	kır	kırdı
dön	döndü	koş	koştu
düş	düştü	tut	tuttu

You must have noticed that the *di* suffix took the form *ti* with the verb "it" (it means push), and likewise **t** has replaced **d** in the suffix with the word düş as well as in the words "at" , "koş" and "tut".
There is a guideline for that, which is written in Table 4.1 below. Don't bother memorizing it because as you speak in Turkish you will naturally veer to the softer t where it applies. It is worth just having an awareness of the guideline.

WHEN WORD ENDS WITH THIS CONSONNANT...	...SUFFIX STARTS WITH THIS LETTER	TURKISH WORD EXAMPLE	ENGLISH MEANING
b	-		
c	(d)		
ç	t	kaçtı	escaped
d	(t)		
f	t	laftı	was words
g	-		
ğ	d	bağdı	was a vine
h	t	ruhtu	was (the) soul
j	(d)	garajdı	was (the) garage
k	t	taktı	hooked, labeled, assigned
l	d	kaldı	stayed, remained
m	d	tamdı	was whole
n	d	döndü	returned, turned
p	t	yaptı	made, built
r	d	kırdı	broke
s	t	kesti	cut
ş	t	koştu	ran
t	t	itti	pushed
v	d	sevdi	liked, loved
y	d	saydı	counted
z	d	yazdı	wrote

TABLE 4.1
Tone Coordination in Suffixes

You may have noticed two things in the above table:

1. Some ending letters have no corresponding suffix consonants, or the consonant is in parenthesis. Those letters are letters in which Turkish words normally do not end; though there may exist exclamations or foreign words in the vocabulary which end that way.
2. Some of the example words are noun forms such as "was (the) garage". Just as in English, in Turkish too you can use the verb "to be" in conjunction with nouns. (We have introduced it here with the Simple Past Tense, equivalent to using "was" in English. Note, however, that the same distinction in form between "was" "became" and "will be", manifests itself in Turkish too. (This is addressed in Chapter 7 – The Verb "to be")

The Present Perfect Form:

Remember that Turkish does not distinguish this form from the Simple Past Form.

The Past Perfect Form:

Once you know the Simple Past Form above you essentially know this form: just use the exact same vowel as the one used in the Simple Past.

    Thus, keeping in sight the rule shown for Simple Past:

use	mişti	where in Simple Past you would use	di or ti
use	müştü	where in Simple Past you would use	dü or tü
use	mıştı	where in Simple Past you would use	dı or tı
use	muştu	where in Simple Past you would use	du or tu

sev	sevmişti		at	atmıştı
it	itmişti		kır	kırmıştı
dön	dönmüştü		koş	koşmuştu
düş	düş müştü		tut	tut muştu

The Future Tense

The Future Tense is one of the simpler ones because its suffix follows the same pattern as the suffix for negation (me, ma) and infinitive (mek, mak). The pattern is:

    The suffix is ecek when the vowel in the root is thin,
    The suffix is acak when the vowel in the root is thick

Let us apply this rule to the words we now know:

sev	sevecek		at	atacak
it	itecek		kır	kıracak
dön	dönecek		koş	koşacak
düş	düşecek		tut	tutacak

The Past Progressive (Future Conditional)

The pattern continues in its simple rendering, where the Future Conditional suffix takes either the form *ecekti* or *acaktı* depending on the root vowel. Hence, once again:

    The suffix is ecekti when the vowel in the root is thin,
    The suffix is acaktı when the vowel in the root is thick

Applying this rule to the words we now know well:

sev	sevecekti	at	atacaktı
it	itecekti	kır	kıracaktı
dön	dönecekti	koş	koşacaktı
düş	düşecekti	tut	tutacaktı

Do you remember the meaning of each of these words? "Sevecekti" means "was going to like".

The Once-Upon-a-Time Form

Same rule here too, where the suffix is either *erdi* or *ardı* :

    The suffix is erdi when the vowel in the root is thin,
    The suffix is ardı when the vowel in the root is thick

Applying this rule to the words we now know well:

sev	severdi	at	atardı
it	iterdi	kır	kırardı
dön	dönerdi	koş	koşardı
düş	düşerdi	tut	tutardı

Note: this form is subject to exceptions and occasionally the suffix takes the form:
    irdi
    urdu
such as in
    gelirdi
    vururdu

These variations follow the pattern of the simple present form, and just as we did then we will leave it wit a simple awareness of its existence.

SUMMARIZING WHAT YOU KNOW SO FAR

You now know all the basic verb forms in Turkish:

- You know the suffixes, tone-coordinated
- You know the negative form of the verb and its tense suffix
- You know the "first person" form of the verb

We shall next look at applying tone coordination to the "first person" suffix.

TONE COORDINATION: THE PERSON

    The rule is universal and similar to that for the Simple Past:

The suffix is *im* or *üm* when the vowel preceding the first person suffix is thin:
  im when the thin vowel is **e** or **i**
  üm when the thin vowel is **ö** or **ü**
The suffix is *ım* or *um* when the vowel preceding the first person suffix is thick:
  dı when the thick vowel is **a** or **ı**
  du when the thick vowel is **o** or **u**

sev	sevdiim	at	attıım
it	ittiim	kır	kırdıım
dön	döndüüm	koş	koştuum
düş	düştüüm	tut	tuttuum

COMBINING SUFFIXES SMOOTHLY

As suffixes tag to the root of the verb and then to one another certain difficult repetition of vowels (such as in the first-person simple past tense – geld*ii*m) or harsh consonant-vowel combinations (such as sevece*ki*m) take place. Turkish, therefore, has simple ways to ease their pronunciation.

We will now quickly see the ways (rules) to easily pronounce these combinations.

1. Where two vowels follow each other drop one (theoretically the 2nd !)

    Example: geldiim   becomes   geldim

2. Where the future tense is used with the negative form do not drop one of the vowels but instead link the two vowels with the letter y .

    Example: gelmeecek   becomes   gelmecek   NOT QUITE
                gelmeecek   becomes   gelme**y**ecek   CORRECT

    This rule, in fact, is an exception to rule 1. (only for the future tense!)

3. Where a vowel follows the letter k replace k with ğ

    Example: gelecekim   becomes   geleceğim

    (remember that ğ is a letter that has no sound of its own but prolongs the sound of the preceding vowel – see Table 1.1)

Let us look at one example using rule 2 and 3 together:

    gelmeecekim   becomes (rule 2)   gelmeyecekim
                        and becomes (rule 3) gelmeyeceğim
which is now the correct form.

NOT ONLY "FIRST PERSON"

We know that, in Turkish, the person is essentially identified by means of a suffix. Remember that the person suffix is the last suffix to be added to the verb.

We know, by now, that to represent the first-person we use the suffix *im* .
Below is the list for all persons:

First Person	**im**
Second Person	**in**
Third Person	*-no suffix-*
First Person Plural	**iz**
Second Person Plural	**iniz**
Third Person Plural	**ler**

Actually a more complete and accurate list would be:

First Person	**im**
Second Person	**in** (when following a vowel), **sin** (following a consonant)
Third Person	*-no suffix-*
First Person Plural	**iz, imiz** (following a consonant), **k** (following a vowel)
Second Person Plural	**iniz** (following a vowel) **siniz** (following a consonant)
Third Person Plural	**ler**

Except for the Third Person Plural, the same tone coordination rules that apply to the first person (refer to the section TONE COORDINATION: THE PERSON in this chapter) also apply to all the others.
The Third Person Plural uses a simplified rule:
    ler   with thin vowels
    lar   with thick vowels

The next page shows examples with the words
    sev   =   like
and   dön   =   turn (return)

Can you complete similar tables with the other words that we learned ? (see the Exercises Booklet – *Exercise 4.15*)

Verb : sev

	Simple Present	Simple Past	Past Peerfect	Future	Future Conditional	Once-Upon-a-Time	Present Continuous	Past Continuous
First Person	severim	sevdim	sevmiştim	seveceğim	sevecektim	severdim	seviyorum	seviyordum
Second Person	seversin	sevdin	sevmiştin	seveceksin	sevecektin	severdin	seviyorsun	seviyordun
Third Person	sever	sevdi	sevmişti	sevecek	sevecekti	severdi	seviyor	seviyordu
First Plural	severiz	sevdik	sevmiştik	seveceğiz	sevecektik	severdik	seviyoruz	seviyorduk
Second Plural	seversiniz	sevdiniz	sevmiştiniz	sevecekseniz	sevecektiniz	severdiniz	seviyorsunuz	seviyordumuz
Third Plural	severler	sevdiler	sevmiştiler[1]	sevecekler	sevecektiler[2]	severdiler[3]	seviyorlar	seviyordular[4]

- In these forms the person suffix leads part of the tense suffix. Good Turkish requires that the words be as follows: 1 sevmişlerdi ; 2 seveceklerdi ; 3 severlerdi ; 4 seviyorlardı

Verb : dön

	Simple Present	Simple Past	Past Perfect	Future	Future Conditional*	Once-Upon-a-Time	Present Continuous	Past Continuous
First Person	dönerim	döndüm	dönmüştüm	döneceğim	dönecektim	dönerdim	dönüyorum	dönüyordum
Second Person	dönersin	döndün	dönmüştün	döneceksin	dönecektin	dönerdin	dönüyorsun	dönüyordun
Third Person	döner	döndü	dönmüştü	dönecek	dönecekti	dönerdi	dönüyor	dönüyordu
First Plural	döneriz	döndük	dönmüştük	döneceğiz	dönecektik	dönerdik	dönüyoruz	dönüyorduk
Second Plural	dönersiniz	döndünüz	dönmüştünüz	döneceksiniz	dönecektiniz	dönerdiniz	dönüyorsunuz	dönüyordumuz
Third Plural	dönerler	döndüler	dönmüşlerdi	dönecekler	döneceklerdi	dönerlerdi	dönüyorlar	dönüyorlardı

* (Past Progressive)

A QUICK LOOK AT TURKISH LETTERS

We are now ready to move on to three forms not yet covered. At that point we will know how to handle just about any verb form and that will put you well beyond half-way to being able to speak basic Turkish.

Before moving on, though, let us quickly look at the complete table of Turkish letters and their sound; we have already seen most of the letters in Lesson 1, Table 1.1.

Turkish letter	Corresponding English letter(s)	sound as in English word:
a	a	art
b	b	
c	dg	ridge
ç	ch	charge
d	d	
e	e	hey (hay) or less
f	f	
g	g	glad
ğ	w	prolongs the preceding vowel as in slowly
h	h	
ı	i	the (as in "the book")
i	i	visit (but maybe closer to he)
j	j	g as in "beau geste"
k	k	
l	l	
m	m	
n	n	
o	o	or
ö	ea	learn , sir
p	p	
		q does not exist
r	r	
s	s	
ş	sh	shame
t	t	
u	oo	foot , who
ü	(u)	Ursula
v	v	
		w does not exist
		x does not exist
y	y	
z	z	

5 TWO NEW FORMS: THE INTERROGATIVE AND THE CONDITIONAL

THE INTERROGATIVE FORM

In Turkish the form that turns a statement into a question or into an interrogative form is the word *mi* .
Since, by now we are familiar with tone coordination we might as well say right away that the interrogative form may really be not only *mi* , but also *mü mı* or *mu* .

To form an interrogative simply follow the verb with the interrogative word *mi mü mı* or *mu* (in fact, as we shall see later, this applies not only to verbs but any kind of word even exclamations).

For example:

    sev   =   like
    sevdim   =   I liked
    sevdim *mi*? =   did I like?

Although the example clearly illustrates the form, it is somewhat of an exception.
Except for the Simple Past Tense, the *mi* inserts itself ahead of the person suffix. In fact not only does it appropriate itself of the person suffix, but it also takes with it the second part of composite tense forms (remember *mişti* ?). This will become clearer to you as you read further on.

We shall look at the different applications of the interrogative with the tenses as well as tone coordination and smooth combination of suffixes.
It would certainly be a good idea to have a quick look at COMBINING SUFFIXES SMOOTHLY in LESSON 4.

Tone Coordination

The interrogative follows the 2nd (complex) form of tone coordination, namely, as for example the Simple Past:

    The interrogative is *mi* or *mü* when the verb has a thin vowel –
        mi when the thin vowel is **e** or **i**
        mü when the thin vowel is **ö** or **ü**
    The interrogative is *mı* or *mu* when the verb has a thick vowel -
        mı when the thick vowel is **a** or **ı**
        mu when the thick vowel is **o** or **u**

sev	sevdi mi?	at	attı mı?
it	itti mi?	kır	kırdı mı?
dön	döndü mü?	koş	koştu mu?
düş	düştü mü?	tut	tuttu mu?

Applying to All Tenses

Applying the interrogative to the different tenses is quite simple.

There are three rules to keep in mind:
1. Tone coordination, as we have seen just above

2. Where composite tenses occur split the tense and add the second part of the composite form to the *mi* .
    Example:

verb root	sev	=	like
Past Perfect	sevmiştim	=	I had liked
composition breakdown			
of Past Perfect	sev mişti im		
where	mişti	is a composit of	miş and di

    Therefore make the interrogative as: sevmiş *mi*dim?
    instead of   sevmistim *mi*?

3. Rule for Combining Suffixes Smoothly: where two vowels follow each other separate them with the letter y (Rule 2 COMBINING SUFFIXES SMOOTHLY in LESSON 4)

    Example:
        interrogative of   severim
        is   sever miyim?

    notice the letter y inserted as follows: sever mi_im

    This smoothing out (for syllable stress reasons) also applies to the connection with the second part of composit verbs. As a result, in practice, the interrogative form *mi* (and *mı mü mu*), except for the Simple Past case, is used with the letter y to effectively become *miy* .

The table below shows all tenses in interrogative form:

	Affirmative	Interrogative	How composed	Smoothing with y	In English
Simple Present	severim	sever miyim	sev*er* mi_im	sever mi*y*im	do I like
Simple Past	sevdim	sevdim mi	--	--	did I like
Past Perfect	sevmiştim	sev*miş* miydim	sev*miş* mi_*di* im	sev*miş* mi*y*dim	had I liked
Future	seveceğim	sevecek miyim	sev*ecek* mi_im	sev*ecek* mi*y*im	will I like
Future Conditional	sevecektim	sevecek miydim	sev*evek* mi_*di* im	sev*ecek* mi*y*dim	was I going to like
Once-Upon-a-Time	severdim	sever miydim	sev*er* mi_*di* im	sev*er* mi*y*dim	did I use to like
Present Continuous	seviyorum	seviyor muyum	sev*iyor* mu_um	sev*iyor* mu*y*um	am I liking
Past Continuous	seviyordum	seviyor muydum	sev*iyor* mu_*du* um	sev*iyor* mu*y*dum	was I liking

THE CONDITIONAL (IF) FORM

We shall now see, in this Basic Book how to form the conditional as it applies to the Simple Present, Simple Past and Future tenses.
Even for these tenses we shall only approach the basic form of the conditional; there are variations giving rich nuances to this form in Turkish. The variations will be shown in the Advanced Book. The present text will limit itself to letting you first get comfortable with the basic knowledge.

The conditional suffix is *se* .

It is placed after the tense – and, as usual, before the person – suffix.
In its basic form it is not compatible with the interrogative form and so only one or the other exists in a word.

For example:
        severim   =   I like
        sever*se*im   =   if I like

But by now we are familiar with the smooth combining of suffixes so we might as well go directly to the smoothened correct form.

Hence the **Simple Present** is:

severseim -> (two vowels following each other: we drop the i to get) seversem

In the case of the Simple Past and the Future we smooth the connection of the tense suffix with the conditional suffix by inserting –the now familiar – letter y .

Hence the **Simple Past**:
    sevdim = I liked
    sevdi*se*im = if I liked   (not smoothed)
    sevdi*yse*m = if I liked   (correct, smoothed form)

Of course you can also have the negative conditional:
    sevdiysem = if I liked
    sev*me*diysem = if I didn't like

And the **Future Tense:**
    seveceğim = I will like
    sevecekseim = if I will like   (not smoothed)
    seveceksem = if I will like   (correct, smoothed form)

The negative conditional of the Future Tense:
    seveceksem = if I will like
    sev*me*yeceksem = if I will not like

And now a quick return to the Simple Present form: (Does this ring a bell?)
Look up in Lesson 2 A QUICK RETURN TO THE SIMPLE PRESENT FORM. We need to quickly look at the negative conditional:
You will see that the negative for the verb
    sev
is, as you know
    sev*me*
When tagged to the negative, the Simple Present tense suffix is of a slightly different form, where, instead of
    er
it takes the form:
    ez
Thus:
    sev = like   (basic form of verb)
    sev*er* = like   (present form, such as in "I like")
    sevme*ez* = not like (such as in "she does not like...")

Well, it is to this very form (negative) that the conditional suffix gets added:

    sevmez = not like
    sevmezse = if not like

sevmezseim	=	if I don't like (not smoothed)
sevmezsem	=	if I don't like (correct, smoothed form)

We have now covered all the basic verb forms.

ONCE AGAIN, WHAT'S NEXT?

If you have a good understanding of what we learned up to now you are very far along knowing how to speak Turkish. There are still certain things you should know before you can really communicate freely, subject to expanding your vocabulary.

What we shall learn next is this:

- Persons: I, you, he-she-it (adverbs).
- Using the verb "to be" and the word "who"
- Using the prepositions "at" "to" "into" "from" "of", the words "this", "that" and the possessive
- The words "who" "what" "where" "when"
- The sequence of words in sentences

At that point we will be able to speak the language. We will then practice making phrases while expanding our vocabulary and learning frequently used phrases.

6 PERSONS

We shall learn the persons and where they are used in Turkish..

THE PERSONS

Ben	=	I
Sen	=	You
O	=	He
		She (as you can see Turkish does not distinguish between these
		It three)
Biz	=	We
Siz	=	You
Onlar	=	They

Note that **Siz**, the plural You, is used not only for plural but also when addressing a person formally, that is, as a **Sen** with distance or respect.

WHERE DO WE USE THE PERSON

Since we have been adding the person as a suffix the question that comes to mind is "where is the person word used?"

One case is **to provide emphasis**

For example we know that:
    geldim = I came
therefore saying:
    ben geldim = I came
has some redundancy. To get a feel for this latter form consider the effect of saying "It is I who came". This, however, is not an actual translation because that level of emphasis has its own corresponding form in Turkish.

The **second use is with the "it is" form of the verb "to be".**
We need the person word in order to be able to say:
    It is I ... *who...*
We shall look at the verb "to be" in just a few moments, in a later chapter.

We also use the person **when grouping**.

For example to say:
> you and me ...

in Turkish:
> sen ve ben ...

(you must have guessed that :
> ve   =   and)

Using *me you him her us them* is treated in Turkish as if using *the I, the you, the he...* and hence will be also addressed in a later chapter.

7 THE VERB "TO BE"

"TO BE" IN TURKISH

The Turkish word for the verb "be" is **ol** .
The negative as you expect is   ol*ma*.

VERB FORMS (TENSES)

The infinitive

We then look at the fundamental verb forms starting with the infinitive:

    ol   =   be
    ol*mak*   =   to be

...And other tenses

But now things get a little complicated.

Remembering how we learned to conjugate *(refer to page 20 of this text)*, and applying it to the verb "be" we should be able to derive the Turkish conjugations as follows:

I am   **olurum**   ol_ur_um   root_tense_person

and similarly with the other persons:

You are   **olursun**   ol_ur_s_un   root_tense_*smoothing*_person
He/She/It is   **olur**
We are   **oluruz**
You are   **olursunuz**
They are   **olurlar**

However, here is the complication:
Although, in the infinitive, *olmak* does translate into "to be" the usual pattern as shown above does not hold for all tenses

So how can we say "be" in other tenses?

The (simple) present tense

Just use the objective form instead of the nominative form of the person – in other words us "me" instead of "I", "her" instead of "she" etc.

For example:

I am at home = (**me** at home) = evde**y**i**m**

The (simple) past tense

I was at home = (**me was** at home) = evde**y**di**m**

The perfect

For the verb "be" use the same form as the simple past – in this case Turkish does not distinguish between these tenses.

The future tense

Here, in Turkish, we do use the word "ol" just as, in English we use the word "be":

I will be at home = evde **olacağım**   ol acak ım

The past progressive (future conditional)

Here too use the word "ol", just as, in English we use the word "be":

I was going to be at home = evde **olacaktım**   ol acaktı ım

The once-upon-a-time form

Again use the "ol" form:

I used to be at home = evde **olurdum**   ol urdu um

The present continuous

For simplicity we will for now say that here too we use the word "ol". But keep in mind that the use of "ol" in this tense becomes context sensitive and, at times, may take on a slightly different meaning than intended: it sometimes means "becoming/getting to be".

But here is the form:

am being = **oluyorum**   ol uyor um

The past continuous

This tense works out the same as the present continuous.
was being = **oluyordum**   ol uyordu um

"To be" can be used in conjunction with :

	verbs	for example:	I am running
with	nouns	for example	I am a lion
or with	adjectives	for example	you are beautiful

In these cases too, in Turkish, one simply uses the objective form:

Verb:
I am running = me (is) running = koşuyorum   koş uyor um

Noun:
I am a lion = me (is) a lion = aslanım   aslan ım

adjective:
you are beautiful = güzelsin   güzel sin

Correct placement of the "to be" suffix

In the prior chapter (6. THE PERSON) we saw the use of the person, such as in
   I am coming

where in Turkish it is

   geliyorum

or, as we just learned could also be

   ben geliyorum

As you can see again, the person is added as a suffix to the verb itself.
Hence you can see that the correct way of saying:
   I am coming
is not   ben**im** geliyor
but   ben geliyor**um**

Use this form with adjectives as well. But note that here too the suffix is connected to the adjective itself rather than the person:
   güzel   =   beautiful
   sen güzel**sin** =   you are beautiful

Note: There exist cases where the "be" suffix (am, are, is) is tagged to the person. For example:
    sen**sin** güzel...   (...güzel sen**sin**)

This however has a very different meaning – dealt with in the Advanced text – and you should, for now avoid tagging the suffix to the person.

(Important: In the "to be" form the syllable stress is on the noun or adjective; the suffix is de-stressed as in:
    GUZELsin
    SENsin

THE REFLECTIVE FORM

In English "be" can reflect on (modify) a verb
    such as in the horse is pushing [the cart]
or can reflect on the object
    such as in the horse is being pushed [by the cart]

Turkish has similar occurences. Thus:
	push is	it
and	be pushed is	itil
	see is	gör
and	be seen is	görün

These examples lead us to list the different forms that the object reflecting takes. These are related to tone coordination and are:

_il

_ıl

_in

_ül

_ün

8 USING THE PREPOSITIONS "at" "to" "into" "from" "of" "with", THE WORDS "This", "That" AND THE POSSESSIVE

USING AN ARTICLE

ADDING, FIRST, WORDS TO OUR - SO FAR - LIMITED VOCABULARY

Let us learn some new Turkish words. This time let us look at nouns.

ev	=	house
ip	=	rope
göl	=	lake
yüz	=	face
at	=	horse
yıl	=	year
kol	=	arm
su	=	water

(remember the verb throw? same phonetics) — next to "at = horse"

THE ARTICLE "A"

The article "a" in Turkish is *bir*. It retains the same form for all words.

bir ev	=	a house
bir ip	=	a rope
bir göl	=	a lake
bir yüz	=	a face
bir at	=	a horse
bir yıl	=	a year
bir kol	=	an arm
bir su ...	=	a water ...

By referring back to CHAPTER 2 THE (SIMPLE) PAST TENSE) and CHAPTER 4 (The Simple Past) you can now say in Turkish:

  A horse ran   =   **Bir at koştu**

THE ARTICLE "THE"

This article takes the form of a suffix, namely, the vowel i, or (depending on tone coordination) $ü$ $ı$ or u.

The suffix is i or $ü$ when the noun has a thin vowel (in its last syllable)–
i when the thin vowel is **e** or **i**
$ü$ when the thin vowel is **ö** or **ü**

The suffix is $ı$ or u when the noun has a thick vowel -
$ı$ when the thick vowel is **a** or **ı**
u when the thick vowel is **o** or **u**

Applying this to our new words:

ev*i*	=	the house
ip*i*	=	the rope
göl*ü*	=	the lake
yüz*ü*	=	the face
at*ı*	=	the horse
yıl*ı*	=	the year
kol*u*	=	the arm
su*yu*	=	the water

Let us note a few things:

Note that "the water" became "su*yu*" instead of su*u*. By now you know that smoothing requires that a "y" to be inserted when the suffix vowel would otherwise immediately follow a vowel.

Turkish does not use the article "the" unless the thing referred to **is a direct object**.
For example, while saying:
    I pushed the horse
Turkish **uses** the article "the":
    At*ı* ittim   (referring back you will recall that ittim is the correct form of
        it_di_im)
However, when saying:
    The horse fell
Turkish **does not use** the article:
    At düştü   (correct form)
    At*ı* düştü   (incorrect form)

Note that in the more common way of forming a phrase the object precedes the verb:
    *At*ı ittim   =   I pushed *the horse*

Here are some examples:
You liked *the horse*	=	Sen *at*ı sevdin	(You *the horse* liked)
You liked *me*	=	Sen ben*i* sevdin	(You *the me* liked)

I liked *you* = Ben sen*i* sevdim   (I *the you* liked)

THE WORDS "this", "that" (and "these", "those")

The Turkish word for "this" is **bu**

Hence:
    this horse = **bu** at

Turkish, though, provides for some nuances: it actually has a second word that means "this". That word is **şu** .
    The difference between **bu** and **şu** is very suttle. It mostly amounts to the difference between pointing to an object and referring to an object as an item under consideration (as if choosing among many). Ther is also a tendency to use **bu** for physical objects and **şu** when referring to a conceptual item. The word **şu** is being mentioned here to create an awareness of it, and, at this stage, it is sufficient to use **bu** in all cases.

Now the Turkish word for "that" is: **o**   (coincidentally same spelling and phonetics as "o" for the third person !)

    that horse = **o** at

Example: o atı gördün mü ?   =   did you see that horse ?

When pointing to more than one item in English we use the words **these** and **those** together with the plural of that item, such as
    these horse**s**
but in Turkish we, regardless, use the singular forms **bu şu o** together with the plural of the item pointed at. This will be explained when we introduce the plural in Chapter 9.

THE "to", "at", "into", "in" AND "from", "with" WORDS

"to" ,"at", "into" and "in" : using "to"

As you've gotten used to by now, here too Turkish uses a suffix.
This suffix for ***to*** is *e* or *a* depending on the vowel of the last syllable of the word.

    The suffix is *e* when the noun has a thin vowel (in its last syllable)–
        whether that vowel be **e i ö** or **ü**
    The suffix is *a* when the noun has a thick vowel -
        ı whether that vowel be **a** or **ı o** or **u**

Applying this to our new words:

ev*e*	=	*to* the house
ip*e*	=	*to* the rope
göl*e*	=	*to* the lake
yüz*e*	=	*to* the face
at*a*	=	*to* the horse
yıl*a*	=	*to* the year
kol*a*	=	*to* the arm
su*ya*	=	*to* the water

Hence:
    at*a* koştum   =   I ran *to* the horse

"to", "at", "into" and "in" : using "at"

The Turkish suffix for **at** is the same as the suffix for *to* and follows the same rules ; but there is one catch:
    This holds true as long as the intended meaning of **at** is "directional", such as when saying: *I looked at the horse* , or *I threw the ball at the dog.*

Hence:
    at*a* baktım = I looked *at* the horse
    topu köpeğ*e* attım = I threw the ball *at* the dog

Let's take this opportunity to make a quick review of our knowledge (and learn two new words):
    top = ball
    köpek = dog

Therefore *to the dog* =   *köpeke* --> no, actually, *köpeğe* (remember Chapter 4 COMBINING SUFFIXES SMOOTHLY)
Also note that in the phrase *at the dog* , the *dog* is not a "direct object" – think of *I threw the ball at the dog* , where the direct object is the *ball*, not the *dog*.
Therefore **the** *dog* does not, in the Turkish expression, receive the suffix **i** (the) and simply remains as *köpek* – and the only suffix "*köpek*" receives is the "e" for "at".

The same applies to pronouns. There is a small deviation from the rule here. The suffix as applied to pronouns is *e* only for "we" and "you" (plural) and otherwise is *a* (and in the process it back-changes the vowel in the pronoun to match:

Here is the list:
    ben   ->   bana   (I -> to (at) me)
    sen   ->   sana

o	->	ona	(smoothing with **n** instead of **y**)
biz	->	bize	
siz	->	size	
onlar	->	onlara	

For example:
    bana koştun   =   you ran to me
you can also say
    sen bana koştun   =   you ran to me (some emphasis on *you*)
    bana attın   =   you threw at me

"to", "at", "in" and "into" : using "in"

We now come to the suffix for *in*.

This suffix is *de* or *da* depending on the vowel of the last syllable of the word.

    The suffix is *de* when the noun has a thin vowel (in its last syllable)–
        whether that vowel be **e i ö** or **ü**
    The suffix is *da* when the noun has a thick vowel -
        ı whether that vowel be **a** or **ı o** or **u**

Applying this to our new words:

    ev*de*   =   *in* the house
    göl*de*   =   *in* the lake

    at*ta*   =   *in* the horse
    yıl*da*   =   *in* the year   or   *[in] a* year
    kol*da*   =   *in* the arm
    su*da*   =   *in* the water

Note: we have seen that the suffix for *at* was *e* as long as *at* was directed *towards* the object. However English uses *at* also to mean *in* such as *I was **at** the house* meaning *I was **in** the house*. When *at* is used in such a context you should use the Turkish suffix *de* just as if the English word *in* (instead of *at*) was being used. In that case:

    I was **at** the house   =   Ben ev*de*ydim
just as:
    ...a dog **in** the house   =   ev*de* bir köpek...

"to", "at", "in" and "into" : using "into"

The word *into* is represented in Turkish by the expression *to the inside of*.

Therefore to say:
> I entered *into* the car

you should think of:
> I entered *to the inside of* the car

And so let us construct the Turkish for *to the inside of:*
First: inside in Turkish is **iç**
Next, recall that *the inside* would therefore be *içi*
Let's now add *to* : the suffix for *to* recall is *e* . *içi* thus becomes *içine* (combining smoothly using "n" -> *içi_e becomes içi_n_e*)

so that we now have an expression for *to the inside* : *içine*

we now need the preposition *of* :

The word "of" is obtained by adding the suffix *in ün ın un* (depending on tone coordination) to the noun or adjective.

Thus *to the inside of...* is *... ın içine*
and *to the inside of the car* is *arabanın içine*

The preposition *of* is explained more just ahead in the text

And now "from"

This suffix is *den* or *dan* depending on the vowel of the last syllable of the word.

> The suffix is *den* when the noun has a thin vowel (in its last syllable)–
> whether that vowel be **e i ö** or **ü**
> The suffix is *dan* when the noun has a thick vowel -
> ı whether that vowel be **a** or **ı o** or **u**

Applying this to our new words:

ev*den*	=	from the house
ip*ten*	=	from the string (rope) or of rope depending on context
göl*den*	=	from the lake
yüz*den*	=	from the face
at*tan*	=	from the horse
yıl*dan*	=	from the year or from year depending on context
kol*dan*	=	from the arm
su*dan*	=	from the water or of water depending on context

The variations and context implications are dealt with in the Advanced Book.

Also note that in some cases (e.g. ip*ten*, at*tan*) the suffix *den* softens as *ten*. (Refer to Table 4.1 on page 22 to briefly review the appropriate lettering).

Example of the use of "from"::
    ev*den* geldim = I came from the house
    yıl*dan* yıl*a* = from year to year   (remember "to" just above)

The same applies to pronouns. But here, unlike the "to-at" form, the root vowel is not changed when using the first (ben) and second (sen) person:

Here is the list:
    ben   ->   benden
    sen   ->   senden
    o   ->   ondan
    biz   ->   bizden
    siz   ->   sizden
    onlar   ->   onlardan

For example:
    benden aldın   =   you took from me
you can also say
    sen benden aldın   =   you took from me (some emphasis on *you*)

going a little further into our knowledge:
    sen onu benden aldın =   you took it from me
    sen onu evden aldın =   you took it from the house

With

The Turkish for "with" is the suffix **le** (**la**)

Example:
    He came with a dog   =   bir köpek**le** geldi

Although this form is perfectly correct at times Turks will use the word **ile** instead of the suffix *le* :

    He came with a dog   =   bir köpek **ile** geldi

We sometimes, in English, add *ed* to a noun to imply *with* and transform the noun into an adjective, for example:
    Salt*ed* fish

In Turkish this takes the form of the suffix **li** (or **lı lu lü**)

Example:
    Salted fish   =   tuz*lu* balık   (tuz = salt ; balık = fish)

However Turks use this same form where "with" is used to combine two things where one is dominant or, say, the second is modified by the first.
For example:
    A man with an umbrella   =   Şemsiye*li* bir adam
    Macaroni with cheese   =   Peynir*li* makarna

This brings us to the word "without". Turkish uses the suffix **siz** (or **sız suz süz**)
    A man without a hat   =   Şapka*sız* bir adam
    A place without water   =   Su*suz* bir yer

THE PREPOSITION "OF"

The word "of" is obtained by adding the suffix *in ün ın un* (depenting on tone coordination) to the noun or adjective.

For example:
ev*in*	=	of the house
ip*in*	=	of the string (rope)
göl*ün*	=	of the lake
yüz*ün*	=	of the face
at*ın*	=	of the horse
yıl*ın*	=	of the year
kol*un*	=	of the arm
su*yun*	=	of the water

Note that this suffix comes after the possession suffix.
For example:
ev*im*	=	my house
ev*in*	=	of the house
ev*imin*	=	of (the) my house

and
at*ın*	=	your horse (coincidentally, could have meant "of the horse" since the "of" suffix is also *ın*)
at*ının*	=	of your horse (technically the **first** *ın* is the "your" and the **second** *ın* is the "of")

THE POSSESSIVE

The possessive suffixes bear some similarity to the person suffixes explained on page 27. It may be a good idea to glance at these suffixes as a background for what is next.

We know by now that to represent the first-person we use the suffix *im*. This applies to the possessive also.
Below is the list for all persons:

First Person	**im**
Second Person	**in**
Third Person	**in, un** (as compared to the *-no suffix-* verb identifyer)
First Person Plural	**im** (with the pronoun) **imiz** (with nouns)
Second Person Plural	**in** (with the pronoun) **iniz** (with nouns)
Third Person Plural	**ın,** (with the pronoun) **i** (with the nouns)

Hence

ben*im*	=	mine
sen*in*	=	yours
o*nun*	=	his, hers, it's (tone coordinated an smoothed with *n*)
biz*im*	=	ours
siz*in*	=	yours
onlar*ın*	=	theirs

and

ev*im*	=	my house
ev*in*	=	your house
ev*i*	=	his, her house
ev*imiz*	=	our house
ev*iniz*	=	your house
ev*i*	=	their house

(sometimes one uses ev*leri* instead of ev*i* even though one is referring to a single house – you will see below that "ler" is normally the plural suffix)

You can now add the "to" to the possessive:

ev*ime*	=	to my house
ev*ine*	=	to your house
ev*ine*	=	to his, her house (here the "n" is for smoothing)
ev*imize*	=	to our house
ev*inize*	=	to your house
ev*lerine*	=	to their house

But if the house is the **direct object** then the suffix becomes *i* instead of *e*.
For example:

evim*i* sevdin	=	you liked my house
evim*e* geldin	=	you came to my house

" HAVE" and "NOT HAVE"

Basically, in Turkish, *have* is expressed with the word **var**.

However, having or not having takes a different turn of phrase in Turkish. Conceptually *have/has* is used as the word *exists*.

For example
    the door of the house   =   evin kapısı

The first thing we notice is that with a possessive (*the door of* as opposed to *the door*) whenever the suffix for "the" (ı) requires a connecting consonant, the connecting consonant used is **s** instead of *y*. Thus:

    door   =   kapı
    the door   =   kapı*y*ı
    the door of...   =   kapı*s*ı...

and so to say:
    the house has a door

you need to think of saying:
    the door of the house exists   =   evin kapısı var
    kapısı   evin   var

Similarly, *not have* is expressed with the word **yok**
For example:
    the house does not have paint =   evin boyası yok

which we get by thinking of the phrase:
    the paint of the house does not exist
    boyası   evin   yok

9 THE PLURAL

THE PLURAL

The plural suffix is *ler* or *lar* (depending on tone coordination)

Thus

ev*ler*	=	houses
ip*ler*	=	strings (ropes)
göl*ler*	=	lakes
yüz*ler*	=	faces
at*lar*	=	horses
yıl*lar*	=	years
kol*lar*	=	arms
su*lar*	=	waters

You can add "the"

ev*leri*	=	the houses
ip*leri*	=	the strings (ropes)
göl*leri*	=	the lakes
yüz*leri*	=	the faces
at*ları*	=	the horses
yıl*ları*	=	the years
kol*ları*	=	the arms
su*ları*	=	the waters

Note that the first suffix added to a noun is the plural.

A LOOK BACK AT "these" and "those"

In Chapter 8 we looked at the words *this* and *that* and saw that when pointing to multiple items even though we would substitute the words *these* and *those* and use them with the plural form if the item. For example:

    this horse -> these horses
    that horse -> those horses

In Turkish we only make the plural of the object. Hence

    bu at -> bu at*lar*
    o at   -> o at*lar*

However, when used without an object, Turkish just as in English does use a plural form of *this* and *that*. And so:

    bunlar   =   these
    onlar   =   those

Example:
    give this to me   =   bana bunu ver   (to me the this give)
    give these to me   =   bana bunları ver   (to me the these give)

10 WHO, WHERE, AND WHAT/WHICH/WHEN/HOW

WHO

The Turkish word for "who" is **kim**.

It is used very much as in English, leading the verb when used with one.

For example:
kim gelir ?	=	who comes ?
kim geldi ?	=	who came ?
kim gelmişti ?	=	who had come ?
kim gelecek ?	=	who will come ?
kim gelecekti ?	=	who was going to come ?
kim gelirdi ?	=	who used to come (would have come) ?

To say "who am I ?" you have to re-sequence the words as:
  I who am ?
and just as we saw in Chapter 7 THE VERB TO BE you add the "to be" part – in this case "am" – to the word **kim**.

and so
who am I ?	=	**ben kimim ?**
who was I ?	=	**ben kimdim ?** (kim di im)
who will I be ?	=	**ben kim olacağım ?** (kim olacak ım)

The "at" "to" and "from" suffixes apply to **kim** just as they apply to nouns (see Chapter 8):

who ... to ?	=	**kime ?**
from whom ?	=	**kimden ?**

For the possessive (whose) simply use the word **kimin.**
whose house ?	=	**kimin evi ?**

WHERE

"Where" follows a very similar pattern to "who".
Just keep in mind that in English "where" is used in conjunction with the verb "to be" and with the prepositions "to" and "from". Hence:

Where (with the verb "be")

where (with the verb "be") = **nerede**

For example:
    where am I ? = **neredeyim**

The tense/forms follow the usual pattern:

where am I ?	=	**neredeyim ?**
where is he/she/it ?	=	**nerede ?**
where was I ?	=	**neredeydim ?**
where had I been ?	=	*use form "where was I?"*
where will I be ?	=	**nerede olacağım ?**

(Note that when saying for example "where is *the house*?" the Turkish form drops "the" such that:
    where is the house ? = **ev nerede ?** (house is where ?))

Where (to):

where (to) = **nereye**

For example:
    where am I going? = **nereye** gidiyorum ?

Where (from)

where (from) = **nereden**

For example:
    where are you coming from? = **nereden** geliyorsun ?

WHAT, WHICH, WHEN, HOW

The Turkish word for "what" is **ne**.

For example:
    what fell ? = **ne düştü**
    what a beautiful house ! = **ne güzel bir ev !**

The Turkish word for "which" is **hangi**.

For example:
    which house ? = **hangi ev ?**
    which book ? = **hangi kitap ?**

and
    which house was it? = **hangi evdi ?**
    which book was it ? = **hangi kitaptı ?**

WHEN

The Turkish for "when" is **ne zaman**.
In fact **ne zaman** stands for "(at) what time".

For example:
    when will you come ? = ne zaman geleceksin ?
    when did she run ? = ne zaman koştu ?

When is not always interrogative and sometimes stands for "at the time that".

In that case only the word **zaman** is used.
For example:
    when I arrived   essentially states "at the time that I arrived"
In Turkish:
    when I arrived = **geldiğim zaman**

HOW

The Turkish word for "how" is **nasıl**.

For example:
    how did you like ? = **nasıl sevdin ?**
    how big ! = **nasıl büyük !**

Do keep in mind that many forms vary from language to language. Treating these nuances are left to the Advanced Text.:
As an example " how much?" in Turkish is *ne kadar ?* as if saying "what amount?"

11 USING YOUR NEW LANGUAGE

SEQUENCING

The typical sequencing, in English, is

SUBJECT	VERB	OBJECT	PREPOSITIONAL PHRASE
I	pushed	the face	of the horse

In Turkish it is

SUBJECT	PREPOSITIONAL PHRASE	OBJECT	VERB (with person suffix)
Ben	atın	yüzünü	ittim

Let us see if we can now form the phrase that we set as an aim (see page 4)

I did not come to the village

SUBJECT	VERB	OBJECT--PREPOSITIONAL PHRASE
I	did not come	to the village

Ben köye gelmedim

SUBJECT	PREPOSITIONAL PHRASE--OBJECT	VERB (with person suffix)
Ben	köye	gelmedim

VOCABULARY

Throughout this text you encountered new words in Turkish. Further down we will make phrases in Turkish – some commonly used and others simply representative of the language.

Before doing that, let us review those words that we have already encountered, as well as introduce some commonly used ones. These, with a reference to where they first were introduced, appear in the table below.

TURKISH	ENGLISH	ALSO MAY MEAN	see page
araba	car ; cart		46
at	horse		41
at	throw		19
balık	fish		47
boya	paint		50
dön	turn ; return		3
düş	fall		19
ev	house		41
gel	come		3
göl	lake		41
güzel	beautiful ; pretty		39
ip	rope ; string		41
it	push	dog (vulgar)	19
kır	break	steer (in a direction)	19
kol	arm		41
koş	run		19
ol	be		52
sev	like ; love		3
su	water		41
tut	hold		19
tuz	salt		47
ve	and		36
yer	place		48
yıl	year	bolt (verb)	41
yüz	face	swim	41

TABLE 11.1
Turkish Words Which Already Appeared in the Text

TURKISH	ENGLISH	ALSO MAY MEAN	see section
al	take ; get		4.4
adam	person		8.4
anla	understand		4.8
çek	pull	suffer	8.2
çıkar	remove		4.8
dükkân	shop		8.8
geç	pass	late	8.1
ger	stretch		8.1
getir	bring		8.10
gir	enter		8.9
git	go		4.8
gör	see		8.1
gün	day		10.6
güneşli	sunny		8.8
işçi	worker		8.4
ne kadar	how much		10.6
kaleci	goalkeeper		8.7
kitap	book		8.7
kız	girl	get angry	8.4
koy	put, place		4.6
kutla	celebrate		8.2
maske	mask		8.4
öde	pay		10.6
pazar	market		8.7
pencere	window		10.6
sakla	hide		8.4
sandal	rowboat		8.8
sene	year		8.1
sor	ask		4.6
sür	drive	spread	8.9
sürdür	make last (time)		4.4
taş	overflow	stone	8.1
top	ball		8.7
toplantı	meeting		10.5
uç	fly	tip ; point	8.10
ver	give		4.6
vur	hit		4.4
yık	demolish ; destroy		8.1
yürü	walk		8.9

TABLE 11.2
Turkish Words Which Appear in the Exercises

ENGLISH	TURKISH	alternative	comment
yes	evet		
no	yok	hayır	'yok' is harsher
I	ben		
you	sen		
he she it	o		
we	biz		
you	siz		also distant or respectful 'sen'
they	onlar		
good morning/afternoon	gün aydın	merhaba	gün = day aydın = bright
good evening	tün aydın	iyi akşamlar	
good night	iyi geceler		iyi = good geceler = nights
good day	iyi günler		'ler' is the plural – like 's'
good bye	allaha ısmarladık		literally: we recommend you to god
thank you	teşekkür ederim	mersi	
thank you very much	çok teşekkür ederim	çok mersi	the 'mersi' form is most commom when used with 'çok'
many thanks	çok teşekkürler		
please	lütfen		
good	iyi		
bad	kötü		
beautiful	güzel		
how pretty	ne güzel		
ugly	çirkin		
dance	dans		
to dance (verb)	dans etmek		
to your health	sıhhatine		plural: sıhhatinize
drink (verb)	iç		
drink (noun)	içki		
wine	şarap		
beer	bira		
water	su		
food	yemek		
come	gel		
go	git		
doing	ediyor		
like (love)	sev		
pleased	memnun		
acceptance	kabul		verb: accept = kabul et

TABLE 11,3
A Review and Some New Turkish Words

MAKING PHRASES

Let us practice making some phrases using what we know:

[you] get me a newspaper

English format

SUBJECT	VERB	PREPOSITION	OBJECT
[you]	get	me	a newspaper

Turkish:

SUBJECT	PREPOSITION	OBJECT	VERB
[sen]	bana	bir gazete	al

the car will stop here

English:
SUBJECT	VERB	PREPOSITION	OBJECT
(the) car	will stop	here	

Turkish:
SUBJECT	PREPOSITION	OBJECT	VERB
araba	burada		duracak

I do not have my document

English
SUBJECT	VERB	PREPOSITION	OBJECT
I (of the me)	do not have		my document

Turkish
SUBJECT	PREPOSITION	OBJECT	(VERB)
benim		belgem	yok

You can now express yourself in Turkish and now all you need is to expand your vocabulary as you go along.
More advanced items are taken up in the Advanced Book.

Exercises and Vocabulary

1 SOME PRINCIPLES OF THE TURKISH LANGUAGE

THE ALPHABET AND SOUND OF THE LETTERS

Review

Review Table 1.1

Exercise 1.1

Write the English letter the phonetics of which corresponds to the Turkish letter in the left column.

Turkish letter	Corresponding English letter(s)
a	
e	
g	
ğ	
ı	
i	
o	
ö	
ş	
u	
ü	

Exercise 1.2

Can you think of an English word that *sounds* similar to the Turkish word in the left column.

Turkish letter	Similar sounding English word
as	
sel	
gam	
dağ	
it	
sor	
şan	
futbol	

VOWELS

Exercise 1.3

In Turkish vowels are broken down into two groups: the *thin vowels* and the *thick vowels*.

(a) Select the thin vowels from the list and write them in the **Turkish vowel** column of the table below

a e ı i o ö u ü

Turkish vowel	Corresponding English letter(s)	

Now write the corresponding English letter(s) in the second column.

(b) Select the thick vowels from the list and write them in the **Turkish Vowel** column of the table below

a e ı i o ö u ü

Turkish vowel	Corresponding English letter(s)	

Now write the corresponding English letter(s) in the second column

PRINCIPLES ABOUT VERBS

Exercise 1.4

Pronounce the Turkish words
Then write the English translation next to them.

    sev   [   ]

    dön   [   ]

    gel   [   ]

Exercise 1.5

(a) Write the negative form of the Turkish word:

    gel   [   ]

(b) Write the simple past tense form of the word:

    gel   [   ]

(c) Now write the simple past tense form of the negative form of the word:

    gel   [   ]

(d) Write the simple past first person form of the word:

    gel   [   ]

(e) Write the negative, simple past, first person form of the word

    gel   [   ]

2 VERBS

THE FUNDAMENTAL FORMS

Exercise 2.1

The word **gel** in Turkish means **come**
In the table below is a list of suffixes used for the different verb forms/tenses

	2 FORM/TENSE	3
gel**di**	....	....
gel**ecek**		
gel**ecekdi**		
gel**er**		
gel**erdi**		
gel**iyor**		
gel**iyordi**		
gel**mek**	infinitive	to come
gel**mişti**		

(a) Complete the **2 FORM/TENSE** column selecting the form/tense from the following list:

infinitive *(already completed)*

simple present   past progressive (future conditional)

simple past /   once-upon-a-time
present perfect

past perfect   present continuous

future   past continuous

(b) Now complete column 3 in English

Exercise 2.2

The word **sev** means **like** in Turkish.

Copy the FORM/TENSE list which you completed in the table of Exercise 2.1 to the same column (column 2) in the table below.

Then complete the table below with the negative of **like (not like)** corresponding to the form/tenses listed in column 2.

1 NOT LIKE	2 FORM/TENSE	3
		did not like
	....	....
		haven't liked
		will not like
		was not going to like
		not like
		not used to like
		not liking
		was not liking
		not to like
		had not liked

Exercise 2.3

(a) What is the suffix that is tagged to a verb to indicate the first person (I)?

(b) Again complete the table below, which is similar to the table in Exercise 2.2 but now includes the first person.

1 NOT LIKE	2 FORM/TENSE	3
	....	I did not like .... haven't liked
		I will not like
		I was not going to like
		I do not like
		I did not use to like
		I am not liking
		I was not liking
	infinitive	not to like
		had not liked

4 REFINING AND BUILDING ON WHAT WE LEARNED

FIRST LET'S REVIEW AND ADD SOME BACKGROUND KNOWLEDGE

As a review let us repeat exercise 1.3

Exercise 1.3

In Turkish vowels are broken down into two groups: the *thin vowels* and the *thick vowels*.

(a) Select the thin vowels from the list and write them in the **Turkish vowel** column of the table below

a   e   ı   i   o   ö   u   ü

Turkish vowel	Corresponding English letter(s)	

Now write the corresponding English letter(s) in the second column.

(b) Select the thick vowels from the list and write them in the **Turkish Vowel** column of the table below

a   e   ı   i   o   ö   u   ü

Turkish vowel	Corresponding English letter(s)	

Now write the corresponding English letter(s) in the second column

Exercise 4.1

(a) Write the English word for the Turkish words listed below.

sev	[	]	[	]
gel	[	]	[	]
it	[	]	[	]
dön	[	]	[	]
düş	[	]	[	]
at	[	]	[	]
kır	[	]	[	]
koş	[	]	[	]
tut	[	]	[	]

Now pronounce the Turkish words relying, when needed, on *Table 1.1*.

(b) Mark, in the second column, whether the vowels in these words are *thin* or *thick (vowels)*

TONE COORDINATION OF SUFFIXES

THE NEGATION SUFFIX

Exercise 4.2

Add the correct **negation suffix** to the following Turkish words:

at___   *not throw*

dön___

düş___

it___

kır___

koş___

sev___

tut___

THE VERB FORMS AND TENSES

Exercise 4.3

Add the correct suffix to form the *infinitive* of the following Turkish words:

at____   *to throw*

dön____

düs____

it____

kır____

koş____

sev____

tut____

Exercise 4.4

(a) Add the correct suffix to form the *simple present* tense of the following Turkish words:

at____   *throw*

dön____

düs____

it____

kır____

koş____

sev____

tut____

(b) The *simple present* suffix for some words takes the less common form   **ir ür ır** or **ur**
Try tagging the correct suffix for the following words:

gel____

vur____   (hit)

al____   (take)

sürdür____   (make last (time))

Exercise 4.5

(a) Add the correct suffix to form the *simple past* tense of the following Turkish words:

at____   *throw*

dön____

düş____

it____

kır____

koş____

sev____

tut____

Exercise 4.6

Add the correct suffix to form the *past perfect* tense of the following Turkish words:

at____   had thrown

dön____

düs____

it____

kır____

koş____

sev____

tut____

gel____

vur____   (hit)

al____   (take)

sürdür____   (make last (time))

ver____   (give)

koy____   (put, place)

sor____   (ask)

Exercise 4.7

Add the correct suffix to form the *future tense* of the following Turkish words:

gel____   will come

vur____   (hit)

al____   (take)

sürdür____   (make last (time)   also drive)

ver____   (give)

koy____   (put, place)

sor____   (ask)

Exercise 4.8

Add the correct suffix to form the *past progressive (future conditional form)* of the following Turkish words:
(Notice the new words with their meaning in parenthesis)

gel_____   was going to come

git_____   (go)

vur_____   (hit)

al_____   (take)

ver_____   (give)

koy_____   (put, place)

çıkar_____   (remove)

sor_____   (ask)

anla_____   (understand)

Exercise 4.9

Add the correct suffix to form the *once-upon-a-time form* of the following Turkish words:
(Notice the new words with their meaning in parenthesis)

gel_____   was going to come

git_____   (go)

vur_____   (hit)

al_____   (take)

ver_____   (give)

koy_____   (put, place)

çıkar_____   (remove)

sor_____   (ask)

anla_____   (understand)

TONE COORDINATION FOR THE PERSON

Exercise 4.10

Write, in the second column of the table below, the first person suffix for a word where the last vowel preceding the suffix is listed in the first column of the table.

last vowel	1st person suffix
a	
e	
ı	
i	
o	
ö	
u	
ü	

Exercise 4.11

Add the correct first person suffix to the past and future tense verbs below:

geldi____

gelecek__

gitti____   (went)

gidecek__   *note the exception: the root is **git -** with the future this word becomes **gid***

vurdu____   (hit)

vuracak__

aldı____   (took)

alacak__

verdi____   (gave)

verecek__

koydu____   (put, placed)

koyacak

çıkardı____   (removed)

çıkaracak

sordu____   (asked)

soracak

anladı____   (understood)

anlayacak__

COMBINING SUFFIXES SMOOTHLY

Exercise 4.12

What are the three rules for combining suffixes smoothly?
Recall that the rules relate to:
- the suffix starts with the same letter as the last one in the word (two vowels follow each other)
- the future tense exception to the first rule
- a vowel follows the (last) letter k

Exercise 4.13

(a) Add the first person suffix to these future tense verbs – making a smooth combination

gelecek__

gidecek__   *note the exception: the root is **git -** with the future this word becomes **gid***

vuracak__

alacak__

verecek__

koyacak__

çıkaracak__

soracak__

anlayacak__

(b) Now first make the negative of the future form and then add the first person to the negative

gelecek

gidecek   *note the exception: the root is **git -** with the future this word becomes **gid***

vuracak

alacak

verecek

koyacak

çıkaracak

soracak

anlayacak

NOT ONLY "FIRST PERSON" : LEARNING ALL PERSONS

Exercise 4.14

Fill in the second column of the table with the suffix for the indicated person.

First person	......	
Second person	....	when following a vowel When following a consonant
Third person (he/ she/ it)	......	
First person plural	....	following a consonant (except in the possessive) following a consonant (in the possessive) following a vowel
Second person plural	....	following a vowel following a consonnant
Third person plural	......	

Exercise 4.15

Complete the table below for all persons combining smoothly the verbs with the person suffix:

	1st person	2nd person	3rd person	1st pers plural	2nd pers plural	3rd pers plural
sevdi	sevdim					
itti	ittim					
döndü	döndüm					
düştü	düştüm					
attı	attım					
kırdı	kırdım					
koştu	koştum					
tuttu	tutum					
sevecek	seveceğim					
itecek	iteceğim					
düşecek	düşeceğim					
atacak	atacağım					
kıracak	kıracağım					
koş	koacağım					
tutacak	tutacağım					

A QUICK LOOK AT TURKISH LETTERS

Exercise 4.16

Find two English words containing the sound of the listed Turkish letter

Turkish letter	English words
a	
c	
ç	
e	
g	
ğ	
ı	
i	
j	
o	
ö	
ş	
u	

5 TWO NEW FORMS: THE INTERROGATIVE AND THE CONDITIONAL

THE INTERROGATIVE FORM

Tone Coordination

In Turkish the form that turns a statement into a question or into an interrogative form is the word *mi* and also *mü mı* or *mu* as required by tone coordination. .

Exercise 5.1 (a)

Write, in the second column of the table below, the English word for the Turkish word appearing in the first column. Write the simple past form of the Turkish word the third column of the table. Then complete the fourth column with the interrogative form of the simple past tense word:

1	2	3	4
sev			
it			
dön			
düş			
at			
kır			
koş			
tut			

Exercise 5.1 (b)

The table below shows the simple present form of the same Turkish words as above. In the adjoining column, write the interrogative form of the word.

1	2
severim	
iterim	
dönerim	
düşerim	
atarım	
kırarım	
koşarım	
tutarım	

Exercise 5.1 (c)

The table below lists, in column 1, the same eight verbs as above. In the adjoining columns, write the interrogative form of the word for the respective tenses as shown.

1	2 PRESENT CONTINUOUS	3 FUTURE
severim	seviyor muyum	sevecek miyim
iterim		
dönerim		
düşerim		
atarım		
kırarım		
koşarım		
tutarım		

Exercise 5.1 (d)

The table below shows the simple present form of the same Turkish words as above. In the adjoining columns, write the interrogative form of the word for the respective tenses shown.

1	2 PAST PERFECT	3 FUTURE CONDITIONAL	4 ONCE-UPON-A-TIME	5 PAST CONTINUOUS
severim	sevmiş miydim	sevecek miydim	sever miydim	seviyor muydum
iterim				
dönerim				
düşerim				
atarım				
kırarım				
koşarım				
tutarım				

Are you able to spot the difference between the forms on table **5.1 (c)** and **5.1 (d)** ?

THE CONDITIONAL (IF) FORM

Exercise 5.2 (a)

The conditional suffix is se
Recall: the simple present for   sev   (like/love)   is   sever
             adding the first person: severim

Write the conditional form of the word severim:

	Affirmative Form	Conditional Form
Simple Present First Person	severim	

Exercise 5.2 (b)

Now write the conditional form of the word for the different tenses:

	Affirmative Form	Conditional Form
Simple Past	sevdim	
Past Perfect	sevmiştim	
Future	seveceğim	
Future Conditional	sevecektim	used in conjunction with the verb "to be"
Once-upon-a-time	severdim	not used
Present Continuous	seviyorum	
Past Continuous	seviyordum	not used

Exercise 5.2 (c)

And now repeat the exercise for the negative form

	Affirmative Form	Negative Conditional Form
Simple Past	sevdim	
Past Perfect	sevmiştim	
Future	seveceğim	
Present Continuous	seviyorum	

6 PERSONS

THE PERSONS

Exercise 6.1

Write the Turkish for:

I	[	]
You	[	]
He	[	]
She	[	]
It	[	]
We	[	]
You	[	]
They	[	]

Exercise 6.2

What are the three main reasons for using the person words in Turkish (given that the person already is evident in the suffix) ?

7 THE VERB "TO BE"

VERB FORMS (TENSES)

Exercise 7.1

List the verb "to be" in Turkish for all persons:

I am	
You are	
He/She/It is	
We are	
You are	
They are	

Exercise 7.2

Write the Turkish for these phrases:

Tense	English form	Turkish form
simple present	**I am** at home	
(simple) past	**I was** at home	
past perfect	*use simple past tense in Turkish*	
future	**I will be** at home	
past progressive	**I was going to be** at home	
once-upon-a-time	**I used to be** at home	
present continuous	**I am being** careful	
past continuous	**I was being** careful	

8 USING ARTICLES "at" "to" "into" "from" "of", THE WORDS "This", "That" AND THE POSSESSIVE

USING AN ARTICLE

THE ARTICLE "A"

Exercise 8.1

Say in Turkish:

A horse ran	:	
A lake overflowed	:	(Turkish for *to overflow* is *taşmak*)
A year passed	:	(Turkish for *pass* is *geç*; *year* is *sene*)
A house was demolished	:	(Turkish for demolish is *yık* and recall that for *be demolished* is *yıkıl*)
A string was stretched	:	(Turkish for *be stretched* is *geril*)
A face was seen	:	(Turkish for *be seen* is *görün*)
An arm was caught	:	(recall Turkish for *catch* is *tut*)

THE ARTICLE "THE"

Exercise 8.2 :

Say in Turkish:

I pulled the horse	:	(Turkish for *pull* is *çek*)
You saw the lake	:	
She celebrated the year	:	(Turkish for *celebrate* is *kutla*)
He painted the house	:	(Turkish for *paint* is *boya*)
We stretched the string	:	
You liked the face	:	
They caught the arm	:	

Exercise 8.3

Write the Turkish for:

    The horse pulled the cart:　　　　　　　　　　　　(Turkish for *cart* is *araba*)

Exercise 8.4

(a) You translated above the phrase:
    "**The** horse pulled **the** cart"　as　--> At arabayı çekti
What is the basis for using the "the" suffix "ı" with the word "araba" (cart) but not with the word "at" (horse) ?

(b) Write the Turkish for:

    Robert saw the lake　　　　:

    Susan celebrated the year　　:

    The worker painted the house :　　　(Turkish for *worker* is *işçi*)

    The girl stretched the string　:　　　(Turkish for *girl* is *kız*)

    The man hid the mask　　　:　　　(Turkish for man is adam
    　　　　　　　　　　　　　　　　　for hide is sakla
    　　　　　　　　　　　　　　　　　for mask is maske)

    The man caught the arm　　:

THE WORDS "this", "that"

Exercise 8.5

(b) Write the Turkish for:

    Robert saw that lake　　　　:

    Susan celebrated this year　:

    The worker painted that house:　　(Turkish for *worker* is *işçi*)

    The girl stretched this string　:　　(Turkish for *girl* is *kız*)

    The man hid that mask　　　:　　(Turkish for man is adam
    　　　　　　　　　　　　　　　　　for hide is sakla
    　　　　　　　　　　　　　　　　　for mask is maske)

    The man caught that arm　　:

THE "to", "at", "into", "in"   AND "from", "of" WORDS

"to", "at", "into" and "in" : using "to"

Exercise 8.6

Write the Turkish word for:

      to the house [   ]

      to the rope [   ]

      to the lake [   ]

      to the face [   ]

      to the horse [   ]

      to the year [   ]

      to the arm [   ]

      to the water [   ]

"to", "at", "into" and "in" : using "at"

Exercise 8.7

Write the following phrases in Turkish:

I ran to the horse   [   ]

He threw the ball at the goalkeeper [   ]
(the Turkish for *goalkeeper* is *kaleci*
the Turkish word for *ball* is *top*)

She gave the book to me [   ]
(the Turkish for *book* is *kitap*)

She threw the book at me [   ]

They went to the market [   ]
(the Turkish for *market* is *pazar*)

"to" ,"at", "into" and "in" : using "in"

Exercise 8.8

Write the following phrases in Turkish:

I was in the car	[ ]	(car: araba)
You were in the shop	[ ]	(shop: dükkân) pronounce as dükyan
He was in Canada	[ ]	(Canada: Kanada)
She was in Turkey	[ ]	(Turkey: Türkiye)
The rowboat was in the lake	[ ]	(rowboat: sandal)
We were in Istanbul	[ ]	(Istanbul: Istanbul)*
You were in a sunny place	[ ]	(sunny: güneşli)
Selim and Nico were in Lausanne	[ ]	(and: ve Lausanne: Lozan)

note that in English the first letter of Istanbul is "i", but in Turkish it is "ı" and is pronounced accordingly.

"to" ,"at", "into" and "in" : using "into"

Exercise 8.9

Write the following phrases in Turkish:

I entered into the car	[ ]	(enter: gir)
You were inside the shop	[ ]	]
He was inside Canada	[ ]	]
She was inside Turkey	[ ]	]
They put the rowboat into the lake	[ ]	]
We were in Istanbul	[ ]	]
You walked into a sunny place	[ ]	(walk: yürü)
Selim and Nico drove into Lausanne	[ ]	(drive: sür)

And now "from"

Exercise 8.10

Write the following phrases in Turkish:

I came from the car	[	]
You came from inside the shop	[	]
He flew from Canada	[	] (*fly: uç*)
She brought it from Turkey	[	] (*bring: getir*)
They took the rowboat from the lake	[	]
We came from Istanbul	[	]
You walked from a sunny place	[	]
Selim and Nico drove from Lausanne	[	]

THE POSSESSIVE

Exercise 8.11

Write the Turkish for:

my house	[	]
your house	[	]
her house	[	]
our house	[	]
your (plural) **house**	[	]
their house	[	]

Exercise 8.12

Write the Turkish for:

mine [ ]

yours [ ]

his [ ]

ours [ ]

yours (plural) [ ]

theirs [ ]

Exercise 8.13

Say in Turkish:

You came to my house [ ]

I came to her house [ ]

I came to your house [ ]

He came to your house [ ]

They will come to our house [ ]

We are coming from their house [ ]

THE PREPOSITION "OF"

Exercise 8.13

(a) Add the appropriate possessive (of) suffix to these words:

ev__

ip__

göl__

yüz__

at__

yıl__

kol__

su___

araba___

boya___

dükkân___

işçi___

kız___

kaleci___

kitap___

yer___

(b) Do you remember the meaning of these words?

9 THE PLURAL

Exercise 9.1

Write the plural:

ev___

ip___

göl___

yüz___

at___

yıl___

kol___

su___

araba___

boya___

dükkân___

işçi___

kız___

kaleci___

kitap___

yer___

Exercise 9.2

Now write the *from* and *to* form :

	PLURAL	FROM	TO
ev	evler		
ip	ipler		
göl	göller		
yüz	yüzler		
at	atlar		
yıl	yıllar		
kol	kollar		
su	sular		
araba	arabalar		
boya	boyalar		
dükkân	dükkânlar		
işçi	işçiler		
kız	kızlar		
kaleci	kaleciler		
kitap	kitaplar		
yerler	yerler		

10 WHO, WHERE, AND WHAT/WHICH/WHEN/HOW

WHO

Exercise 10.1

Write the Turkish expression for:

- who comes ?   [   ]
- who came ?   [   ]
- who had come ?   [   ]
- who will come ?   [   ]
- who was going to come ?   [   ]
- who used to come (would have come) ? [   ]

Exercise 10.2

Write the Turkish expression for:

- who am I ?   [   ]
- who was I ?   [   ]
- who will I be ? [   ]

Exercise 10.3

Write in Turkish :

- who ... to ?   [   ]
- from whom ?   [   ]
- whose house ?   [   ]

Exercise 10.4

Write the following expressions in Turkish:

Who is coming to the house ?　　　　　　　　[　　　　　　　　　　　　]
to the house who is coming

Who threw the ball at the house ?　　　　　　[　　　　　　　　　　　　]
at the house who the ball threw

Who is bringing the boat to the lake ?　　　　[　　　　　　　　　　　　]
to the lake who the boat is bringing

WHERE

Exercise 10.5

Write the Turkish for:

Where is the meeting ?　　　　　[　　　　　　　　　　　] (*meeting: toplantı*)

Where will they bring the boat [to] ?　[　　　　　　　　　　　]

Where did they bring the boat from ? [　　　　　　　　　　　]

WHAT, WHICH, WHEN, HOW

Exercise 10.6

Write these phrases in Turkish:

What did they bring to the lake ?　　　　[　　　　　　　　　　　　]

What did the horse do ?　　　　　　　　　[　　　　　　　　　　　　]

Which animal is in the farm ?　　　　　　[　　　　　　　　　　　　]

What fell from the window of the house ?　[　　　　　　　　　　　　]
　　　(*window : pencere*)
Which window of the house ?　　　　　　[　　　　　　　　　　　　]
　　　(*of the house which [the]window ?*)
When did it fall ?　　　　　　　　　　　[　　　　　　　　　　　　]

When are you coming to my house ?　　　[　　　　　　　　　　　　]
　　　(*to my house when are you coming*)
What day will you be coming to my house ? [　　　　　　　　　　　　]
　　　(*day : gün*)
Which day will you come to my house ?　　[　　　　　　　　　　　　]

How will you come to my house ? [   ]

How much did you run ? [   ]
   (*much (in this context): kadar*)

How much did you pay ? [   ]
   (pay : öde)

Answers to Exercises

1 SOME PRINCIPLES OF THE TURKISH LANGUAGE

THE ALPHABET AND SOUND OF THE LETTERS

Exercise 1.1

Turkish letter	Corresponding English letter(s)	sounds as in English word:
a	a	art
e	e	hey (hay) or less
g	g	glad
ğ	w	prolongs the preceding vowel as in slowly
ı	i	the (as in "the book")
i	i	visit (but maybe closer to he)
o	o	or
ö	ea	learn, sir
ş	sh	shame
u	oo	foot, who
ü	(u)	Ursula

Exercise 1.2

Turkish letter	Similar sounding English word	By the way the Turkish word means:
as	us	*hang*
sel	sell	*heavy rain, flood*
gam	gum	*grieve*
dağ	duh	*mountain*
it	eat	*push*
sor	sore	*ask*
şan	shun	*glory*
futbol	football	*soccer*

Exercise 1.3

(a)

Turkish vowel (thin)	Corresponding English letter(s)	
e	e	
i	i	
ö	ea	
ü	(u)	

(b)

Turkish vowel (thick)	Corresponding English letter(s)	
a	a	
ı	i (see Table 1.1)	
o	o	
u	oo	

PRINCIPLES ABOUT VERBS

Exercise 1.4

sev	[	like (love)]
dön	[	turn (return)]
gel	[	come]

Exercise 1.5

(a) negative form:

| gel | [| **gelme**] |

(b) simple past tense:

| gel | [| **geldi**] |

(c) simple past tense form of the negative form:

| gel | [| **gelmedi**] |

(d) simple past first person:

| gel | [| geldiim] |

(e) negative, simple past, first person form:

| gel | [| gelmediim] |

2 VERBS

THE FUNDAMENTAL FORMS

Exercise 2.1

	2 FORM/TENSE	3
geldi	simple past .... present perfect	came .... has come
gelecek	future	will come
gelecekdi	past progressive (future conditional)	was going to come
geler	simple present	come
gelerdi	once-upon-a-time	used to come
geliyor	present continuous	coming
geliyordi	past continuous	was coming
gelmek	infinitive	to come
gelmişti	past perfect	had come

Exercise 2.2

1 NOT LIKE	2 FORM/TENSE	3
sevmedi	simple past	did not like
	present perfect	haven't liked
sevmeecek	future	will not like
sevmeecekdi	past progressive (future conditional)	was not going to like
sevme	simple present	not like
sevmeezdi	once-upon-a-time	not used to like
sevmeiyor	present continuous	not liking
sevmeiyordi	past continuous	was not liking
sevmemek	infinitive	not to like
sevmemişti	past perfect	had not liked

Exercise 2.3

(a) the suffix that is tagged to a verb to indicate the first person is **im**

(b)

1 NOT LIKE	2 FORM/TENSE	3
sevmediim	simple past .... present perfect	I did not like .... haven't liked
sevmeecekim	future	I will not like
sevmeecekdiim	past progressive (future conditional)	I was not going to like
sevmem	simple present	I do not like
sevmeezdiim	once-upon-a-time	I did not use to like
sevmeiyorim	present continuous	I am not liking
sevmeiyordiim	past continuous	I was not liking
sevmemek	infinitive	not to like
sevmemiştiim	past perfect	had not liked

4 REFINING AND BUILDING ON WHAT WE LEARNED

FIRST LET'S REVIEW AND ADD SOME BACKGROUND KNOWLEDGE

Exercise 1.3 (repeat)

(a)

Turkish vowel	Corresponding English letter(s)	
e	e	
i	i	
ö	ea	
ü	(u)	

(b)

Turkish vowel	Corresponding English letter(s)	
a	a	
ı	i	
o	o	
u	oo	

Exercise 4.1

	(a)			(b)	
sev	[	like (love)	]	[thin	]
gel	[	come	]	[thin	]
it	[	push	]	[thin	]
dön	[	turn (return)	]	[thin	]
düş	[	fall	]	[thin	]
at	[	throw	]	[thick	]
kır	[	break	]	[thick	]
koş	[	run	]	[thick	]
tut	[	catch	]	[thick	]

TONE COORDINATION OF SUFFIXES

THE NEGATION SUFFIX

Exercise 4.2

at<u>ma</u>

dön<u>me</u>

düş<u>me</u>

it<u>me</u>

kır<u>ma</u>

koş<u>ma</u>

sev<u>me</u>

tut<u>ma</u>

THE VERB FORMS AND TENSES

Exercise 4.3

the infinitive

atmak

dönmek

düşmek

itmek

kırmak

koşmak

sevmek

tutmak

Exercise 4.4

(a) *The simple present*

atar

döner

düşer

iter

kırar

koşar

sever

tutar

(b) *The simple present* with the less common form ir ür ır or ur

gelir	(come)
vurur	(hit)
alır	(take)
sürdürür	(make last (time))

Exercise 4.5

(a) *The simple past*

attı

döndü

düştü

itti

kırdı

koştu

sevdi

tuttu

Exercise 4.6

The past perfect

atmıştı

dönmüştü

düşmüştü

itmişti

kırmıştı

koşmuştu

sevmişti

tutmuştu

gelmişti   (had come)

vurmuştu   (had hit)

almıştı   (had taken)

sürdürmüştü   (had made last (time))

vermişti   (had given)

koymuştu   (had put, had placed)

sormuştu   (had asked)

Exercise 4.7

The future tense

gelecek	(will come)
vuracak	(will hit)
alacak	(take)
sürdürecek	(will make last (time))
verecek	(will give)
koyacak	(will put, will place)
soracak	(will ask)

Exercise 4.8

The past progressive (future conditional form)

gelecekti	(was going to come)
vuracaktı	(was going to hit)
alacaktı	(was going to take)
sürdürecekti	(was going to make last (time)) ; also (was going to make drive)
verecekti	(was going to give)
koyacaktı	(was going to put, was going to place)
soracaktı	(was going to ask)
anlaacaktı	(was going to understand)

Exercise 4.9

The once-upon-a-time form

gelirdi	(used to come)
vururdu	(used to hit)
alırdı	(used to take)
sürdürürdü	(used to make last (time))
verirdi	(used to give)
koyardı	(used to put, used to place)
sorardı	(used to ask)
anlaardı	(used to understand)

TONE COORDINATION FOR THE PERSON

Exercise 4.10

last vowel	1st person suffix
a	ım
e	im
ı	ım
i	im
o	um
ö	üm
u	um
ü	üm

Exercise 4.11

geldiim

gelecekim

gittiim

gidecekim

vurduum

vuracakım

aldıım

alacakım

verdiim

verecekim

koyduum

koyacakım

çıkardıım

çıkaracakım

sorduum

soracakım

anladıım

anlayacakım

COMBINING SUFFIXES SMOOTHLY

Exercise 4.12

What are the three rules for combining suffixes smoothly?

1. Where two vowels follow each other drop one (theoretically the 2nd !)

   Example: geldiim   becomes   geldim

2. Where the future tense is used with the negative form do not drop one of the vowels but instead link the two vowels with the letter y .

   Example: gelmeecek   becomes   gelmecek   *WRONG*
   gelmeecek   becomes   gelmeyecek   *CORRECT*

   This rule, in fact, is an exception to rule 1. (only for the future tense!)

3. Where a vowel follows the letter k replace k with ğ

   Example: gelecekim   becomes   geleceğim

   (remember that ğ is a letter that has no sound of its own but prolongs the sound of the preceding vowel – see TABLE 1.1)

Exercise 4.13

(a) Add the first person suffix to these future tense verbs – making a smooth combination

geleceğim

gideceğim   *note the exception: the root is git - with the future this word becomes gid*

vuracağım

alacağım

vereceğim

koyacağım

çıkaracağım

soracağım

anlayacağım

(b) Now first make the negative of the future form and then add the first person to the negative

gelmeyeceğim

gitmeyeceğim   *note the exception condition does not apply in the negative form*

vurmayacağım

almayacağım

vermeyeceğim

koymayacağım

çıkarmayacağım

sormayacağım

anlamayacağım

NOT ONLY "FIRST PERSON" : LEARNING ALL PERSONS

Exercise 4.14

First person	im......	
Second person	in.....	when following a vowel
	sin.....	When following a consonant
Third person (he/ she/ it)	.-....	
First person plural	iz.....	following a consonant (except in the possessive)
	imiz.....	following a consonant (in the possessive)
	k.....	following a vowel
Second person plural	iniz.....	following a vowel
	siniz.....	following a consonnant
Third person plural	ler.....	

Exercise 4.15

Complete the table below for all persons combining smoothly the verbs with the person suffix:

	1st person	2nd person	3rd person	1st pers plural	2nd pers plural	3rd pers plural
sevdi	sevdim	sevdin	sevdi	sevdik	sevdiiniz	sevdiler
itti	ittim	ittin	itti	ittik	ittiiniz	ittiiler
döndü	döndüm	döndün	döndü	döndük	döndünüz	döndüler
düştü	düştüm	düştün	düştü	düştük	düştünüz	düştüler
attı	attım	attın	attı	attık	attınız	attılar
kırdı	kırdım	kırdın	kırdı	kırdık	kırdınız	kırdılar
koştu	koştum	koştun	koştu	koştuk	koştunuz	koştular
tuttu	tutum	tutun	tutu	tutuk	tutunuz	tutular
sevecek	seveceğim	seveceksin	sevecek	seveceğiz	sevecesiniz	sevecekler
itecek	iteceğim	iteceksin	itecek	iteceğiz	iteceksiniz	itecekler
düşecek	düşeceğim	düşeceksin	düşecek	düşeceğiz	düşeceksiniz	düşecekler
atacak	atacağım	atacağım	atacak	atacağız	atacaksınız	atacaklar
kıracak	kıracağım	kırcağım	kıacak	kıracağız	kıracaksınız	kıracaklar
koş	koşacağım	koşacaksın	koşacak	koşacağız	koşacaksınız	koşacaklar
tutacak	tutacağım	ktutacaksın	ktutacak	tutacağız	tutacaksınız	tutacaklar

Exercise 4.16

Turkish letter	English words	alternative with same sound
a	art, past	must
c	jam, reject	ridge
ç	charge, chimney	ratchet
e	hey, escapade	hay
g	glad, ground	
ğ	slowly, law	
ı	the	
i	visit, impossible	he
j	regime, geste (in French)	
o	or, ordeal	
ö	learn, turn	sir
ş	shame, rush	
u	foot, look	who

5 TWO NEW FORMS: THE INTERROGATIVE AND THE CONDITIONAL

THE INTERROGATIVE FORM

Exercise 5.1 (a)

1	2	3	4
sev	like (love)	sevdi	sevdi mi?
it	push	itti	itti mi?
dön	turn (return)	döndü	döndü mü?
düş	fall	düştü	düştü mü?
at	throw	attı	attı mı?
kır	break	kır	kırdı mı?
koş	run	koş	koştu mu?
tut	catch	tut	tuttu mu?

Exercise 5.1 (b)

1	2
severim	sever miyim
iterim	iter miyim
dönerim	döner miyim
düşerim	düşer miyim
atarım	atar mıyım
kırarım	kırar mıyım
koşarım	koşar mıyım
tutarım	tutar mıyım

Exercise 5.1 (c)

1	2 PRESENT CONTINUOUS	3 FUTURE
severim	seviyor muyum	sevecek miyim
iterim	itiyor muyum	itecek miyim
dönerim	dönüyor muyum	dönecek miyim
düşerim	düşüyor muyum	düşecek miyim
atarım	atıyor muyum	atacak mıyım
kırarım	kırıyor muyum	kıracak mıyım
koşarım	koşuyor muyum	koşacak mıyım
tutarım	tutuyor muyum	tutacak mıyım

Exercise 5.1 (d)

1	2 PAST PERFECT	3 FUTURE CONDITIONAL	4 ONCE-UPON-A-TIME	5 PAST CONTINUOUS
severim	sevmiş miydim	sevecek miydim	sever miydim	seviyor muydum
iterim	itmiş miydim	itecek miydim	iter miydim	itiyor muydum
dönerim	dönmüş müydüm	dönecek miydim	döner miydim	dönüyor muydum
düşerim	düşmüş müydüm	düşecek miydim	düşer miydim	düşüyor muydum
atarım	atmış mıydım	atacak mıydım	atar mıydım	atıyor muydum
kırarım	kırmış mıydım	kıracak mıydım	kırar mıydım	kırıyor muydum
koşarım	koşmuş muydum	koşacak mıydım	koşar mıydım	koşuyor muydum
tutarım	tutmuş muydum	tutacak mıydım	tutar mıydım	tutuyor muydum

Are you able to spot the difference between the forms on table **5.1 (c) and 5.1 (d)** ?

The tenses in table 5.1 (d) are composites. Thus the first person past perfect form of *sev* is *sevmiştim* where the tense suffix *misti* can be construed as being a composite of *miş* and *di* to form *mişti*.

Similarly the first person future conditional suffix is composed of *ecek* and *di* to form *ecekti* with the *im* first person suffix tagged onto ecekti to form *ecektiim* and, dropping one of the i's, *ecektim*.

In these cases the interrogative form suffix *mi* (or *mı, mu, mü*) is positioned after the first part of the composite tense suffix and before the second part of the suffix

Hence instead of saying: *sevmiştim mi* we say *sevmiş miydim (sev_mişti_im mi -> sev_miş mi_ di_im)*

THE CONDITIONAL (IF) FORM

Exercise 5.2 (a)

The conditional form of the word severim:

	Affirmative Form	Conditional Form
Simple Present First Person	severim	seversem

Exercise 5.2 (b)

The conditional form of the word for the different tenses:

	Affirmative Form	Conditional Form
Simple Past	sevdim	sevdiysem (sevdimse)
Past Perfect	sevmiştim	sevmişsem
Future	seveceğim	seveceksem
Future Conditional	sevecektim	used in conjunction with the verb "to be"
Once-upon-a-time	severdim	not used
Present Continuous	seviyorum	seviyorsam
Past Continuous	seviyordum	not used

Exercise 5.2 (c)

The negative conditional form

	Affirmative Form	Negative Conditional Form
Simple Past	sevdim	sevmediysem (sevmedimse)
Past Perfect	sevmiştim	sevmemişsem
Future	seveceğim	sevmeyeceksem
Present Continuous	seviyorum	sevmiyorsam

6 PERSONS

Exercise 6.1

Write the Turkish for:

I	[ben	]
You	[sen	]
He	[o	]
She	[o	]
It	[o	]
We	[biz	]
You	[siz	]
They	[onlar	]

Exercise 6.2

The three main reasons for using the person in Turkish :

.1   to provide emphasis
.2   to use is with the "it is" form of the verb "to be".
        We need the person word in order to be able to say:
        It is I ... *who*...
.3   when grouping.
        For example to say:
            you and me ...
        in Turkish:
            sen ve ben ...
        (you must have guessed that :
            ve = and)

7 THE VERB "TO BE"

VERB FORMS (TENSES)

Exercise 7.1

The verb "to be" in Turkish for all persons:

I am	olurum
You are	olursun
He/She/It is	olur
We are	oluruz
You are	olursunuz
They are	olurlar

Exercise 7.2

Tense	English form	Turkish form
simple present	I am at home	evdeyim
(simple) past	I was at home	evdeydim
past perfect	*use simple past tense in Turkish*	
future	I will be at home	evde olacağım
past progressive	I was going to be at home	evde olacaktım
once-upon-a-time	I used to be at home	evde olurdum
present continuous	I am being careful	dikkatli oluyorum
past continuous	I was being careful	dikkatli oluyordum

8 USING ARTICLES "at" "to" "into" "from" "of", THE WORDS "This", "That" AND THE POSSESSIVE

USING AN ARTICLE

THE ARTICLE "A"

Exercise 8.1

Say in Turkish:

A horse ran	:	**Bir** at koştu
A lake overflowed	:	**Bir** göl taştı
A year passed	:	**Bir** sene geçti
A house was demolished:		**Bir** ev yıkıldı
A string was stretched :		**Bir** ip gerildi
A face was seen	:	**Bir** yüz göründü
An arm was caught	:	**Bir** kol tutuldu

THE ARTICLE "THE"

Exercise 8.2 :

Say in Turkish:

I pulled **the** horse	:	At**ı** çektim
You saw **the** lake	:	Göl**ü** gördün
She celebrated **the** year:		Yıl**ı** kutladı
He painted **the** house	:	Ev**i** boyadı
We stretched **the** string:		İp**i** gerdik
You liked **the** face	:	Yüz**ü** sevdiniz
They caught **the** arm	:	Kol**u** tuttular

Exercise 8.3

Write the Turkish for:

    The horse pulled the cart: At arabayı çekti

Exercise 8.4

(a) The basis for using the "the" suffix "ı" with the word "araba" but not with the word "at"

The article "the" is only used with a (direct) object

(b) The Turkish for:

Robert saw the lake	:	Robert gölü gördü
Susan celebrated the year	:	Susan yılı kutladı
The worker painted the house	:	İşçi evi boyadı
The girl stretched the string	:	Kız ipi gerdi
The man hid the mask	:	Adam maskeyi sakladı
The man caught the arm	:	Adam kolu tuttu

THE WORDS "this", "that"

Exercise 8.5

The Turkish for:

Robert saw that lake	:	Robert **o** gölü gördü
Susan celebrated this year	:	Susan **bu** yılı kutladı
The worker painted that house	:	İşçi **o** evi boyadı
The girl stretched this string	:	Kız **şu** ipi gerdi
The man hid that mask	:	Adam **o** maskeyi sakladı
The man caught that arm	:	Adam **o** kolu tuttu

THE "to", "at", "into", "in"   AND   "from", "of" WORDS

"to", "at", "into" and "in" : using "to"

Exercise 8.6

The Turkish word for:

to the house	[eve]
to the rope	[ipe]
to the lake	[göle]
to the face	[yüze]
to the horse	[ata]
to the year	[yıla]
to the arm	[kola]
to the water	[suya]

"to", "at", "into" and "in" : using "at"

Exercise 8.7

Phrases in Turkish:

I ran to the horse	[Ata koştum]
He threw the ball at the goalkeeper (the Turkish for *goalkeeper* is *kaleci*)	[Topu kaleciye attı]
She gave the book to me (the Turkish for *book* is *kitap*)	[Kitabı bana verdi]
She threw the book at me	[Kitabı bana attı]
They went to the market (the Turkish for *market* is *pazar*)	[Pazara gittiler]

"to", "at", "into" and "in" : using "in"

Exercise 8.8

Write the following phrases in Turkish:

I was in the car	[Arabadaydım (or ben arabadaydım)]
You were in the shop	[Dükkândaydın (or sen dükkândaydın)]
He was in Canada	[Kanadadaydı (or o Kanadadaydı]
She was in Turkey	[Türkiyedeydi (or o Türkiyedeydi]
The boat was in the lake	[Sandal göldeydi]
We were in Istanbul	[Istanbuldaydık (or biz Istanbuldaydık]
You were in a sunny place	[Güneşli bir yerdeydiniz]
Selim and Nico were in Lausanne	[Selim ve Niko Lozandaydılar]

"to", "at", "into" and "in" : using "into"

Exercise 8.9

Write the following phrases in Turkish:

I entered into the car	[Arabanın içine girdim]
You were inside the shop	[Dükkânın içindeydin]
He was inside Canada	[Kanadanın içindeydi]
She was inside Turkey	[Türkiyenin içindeydi]
They put the rowboat into the lake	[Sandalı gölün içine koydular]
We were inside Istanbul	[Istanbulun içindeydik]
You walked into a sunny place	[Güneşli bir yerin içine yürüdünüz]
Selim and Nico drove into Lausanne	[Selim ve Niko Lozanın içine sürdüler]

And now "from"

Exercise 8.10

Write the following phrases in Turkish:

I came from the car	[Arabadan geldim]
You came from inside the shop	[Dükkânın içinden geldin]
He flew from Canada	[Kanadadan uçtu]
She brought it from Turkey	[Türkiyeden getirdi]
They took the rowboat from the lake	[Sandalı gölden aldılar]
We came from Istanbul	[Istanbuldan geldik]
You walked from a sunny place	[Güneşli bir yerden yürüdün]
Selim and Nico drove from Lausanne	[Selim ve Niko Lozandan sürdüler]

THE POSSESSIVE

Exercise 8.11

Write the Turkish for:

my house	[evim]
your house	[evin]
her house	[evi]
our house	[evimiz]
your (plural) house	[eviniz]
their house	[evi]

Exercise 8.12

Write the Turkish for:

mine	[benim]
yours	[senin]
his	[onun]
ours	[bizim]

| yours (plural) | [sizin] |
| theirs | [onların] |

Exercise 8.13

Say in Turkish:

You came to my house	[evime geldin]	
I came to her house	[evine geldim]	evi_n_e gel_di_im *
I came to your house	[evine geldim]	evin_ _e gel_di_im *
He came to your house	[evine geldi]	
They will come to our house	[evimize gelecekler]	
We are coming from their house	[evlerinden geliyoruz]	

* In both expressions the Turkish form is identical – but it is a coincidence: *her house* is *evi* and *your house* is *evin*. To add *to* we add the suffix *e* so that *to her house* becomes *evi_e* and *to your house* becomes *evin_e*. However *evi_e* has to be smoothed and also ends up as *evi_n_e* !

Exercise 8.14

(a)..........	(b)........
ev**in**	house
ip**in**	rope
göl**ün**	lake
yüz**ün**	face
at**ın**	horse
yıl**ın**	year
kol**un**	arm
su**yun** *note the exception: smoothing is letter is "y"*	water
araba**nın**	car, cart
boya**nın**	paint
dükkân**ın**	shop
işçi**nin**	worker
kız**ın**	girl

kalecinin   goalkeeper

kitabın   *note the exception:*   book
  "p" is changed to the easier to pronounce "b"
yerin   place

9 THE PLURAL

Exercise 9.1

Write the plural:

evler

ipler

göller

yüzler

atlar

yıllar

kollar

sular

arabalar

boyalar

dükkânlar

işçiler

kızlar

kaleciler

kitaplar

yerler

Exercise 9.2

	PLURAL	FROM	TO
ev	evler	evlerden	evlere
ip	ipler	iplerden	iplere
göl	göller	göllerden	göllere
yüz	yüzler	yüzlerden	yüzlere
at	atlar	atlardan	atlara
yıl	yıllar	yıllardan	yıllara
kol	kollar	kollardan	kollara
su	sular	sulardan	sulara
araba	arabalar	arabalardan	arabalara
boya	boyalar	boyalardan	boyalara
dükkân	dükkânlar	dükkânlardan	dükkânlara
işçi	işçiler	işçilerden	işçilere
kız	kızlar	kızlardan	kızlara
kaleci	kaleciler	kalecilerden	kalecilere
kitap	kitaplar	kitaplardan	kitaplara
yerler	yerler	yerlerden	yerlere

10 WHO, WHERE, AND WHAT/WHICH/WHEN/HOW

WHO

Exercise 10.1

Write the Turkish expression for:

who comes ?	[kim gelir ?]
who came ?	[kim geldi ?]
who had come ?	[kim gelmişti ?]
who will come ?	[kim gelecek ?]
who was going to come ?	[kim gelecekti ?]
who used to come (would have come) ?	[kim gelirdi ?]

Exercise 10.2

Write the Turkish expression for:

who am I ?	[ben kimim ?]
who was I ?	[ben kimdim ?]
who will I be ?	[ben kim olacağım ?]

Exercise 10.3

Write in Turkish :

who ... to (to whome)?	[kime ?]
from whom ?	[kimden ?]
whose (house) ?	[kimin (evi) ?]

Exercise 10.4

Write the following expressions in Turkish:

Who is coming to the house ? [Eve kim geliyor ?]
  to the house who is coming

Who threw the ball at the house ? [Eve kim topu attı ?]
  at the house who the ball threw

Who is bringing the boat to the lake ? [Göle kim sandalı getiriyor ?]
  : to the lake who the boat is bringing

WHERE

Exercise 10.5

Write the Turkish for:

Where is the meeting ? [Toplantı nerede ?]
Where will they bring the boat [to] ? [Sandalı nereye getirecekler ?]
Where did they bring the boat from ? [Sandalı nereden getirdiler ?]

WHAT, WHICH, WHEN, HOW

Exercise 10 6

Phrases in Turkish

What did they bring to the lake ? [Göle nw getirdiler ?]
What did the horse do ? [At ne yaptı ?]
Which animal is in the farm ? [Hangi hayvan çiftliktedir ?]
What fell from the window of the house ? [Evin penceresinden ne düştü ?]
  (window : pencere)
Which window of the house ? [Evin hangi penceresi ?]
  (of the house which [the]window ?)
When did it fall ? [Ne zaman düştü ?]
When are you coming to my house ? [Evime ne zaman geliyorsun ?]
  (to my house when are you coming)
What day will you be coming to my house ? [Evime ne gün geleceksin ?] *
  (day : gün)
Which day will you come to my house ? [Evime hangi gün geleceksin ?] *

How will you come to my house ?   [Evime nasıl geleceksin ?   ]

How much did you run ?   [Ne kadar koştun ?   ]
    (*much (in this context): kadar*)

How much did you pay ?   [Ne kadar ödedin ?   ]
(pay : öde)

* You notice that "will you be coming" and "will you come" have the same form in Turkish. Note that there is a form close to the "will be coming" which is distinct from the "will come" form. That form essentially reproduces "will be in the process of coming" and therefore translates as "evime ne gün gelmekte olacaksın ?". This form, though is not best suited to this context; therefore, at this stage, just have an awareness of its existence.